GUYANA

CHAITRAM SINGH

Copublished with Hoover Institution Press,
Stanford University, Stanford, California

POLITICS IN LATIN AMERICA
A HOOVER INSTITUTION SERIES

General Editor, **Robert Wesson**

GUYANA

Politics in a Plantation Society

Chaitram Singh

PRAEGER

New York
Westport, Connecticut
London

Library of Congress Cataloging-in-Publication Data

Singh, Chaitram.
    Guyana : politics in a plantation society.

    (Politics in Latin America)
    Bibliography: p.
    Includes index.
    1. Guyana—Politics and government—1966–
I. Title. II. Series.
F2385.S56 1988   988'.103   87–38484
ISBN 0–275–92989–2 (alk. paper)

Library of Congress Catalog Card Number: 87–38484

ISBN: 0–275–92989–2

First published in 1988

Praeger Publishers, One Madison Avenue, New York, NY 10010
A division of Greenwood Press, Inc.

Printed in the United States of America

The paper used in this book complies with the
Permanent Paper Standard issued by the National
Information Standards Organization (Z39.48–1984).

10 9 8 7 6 5 4 3 2 1

For Kathy

CONTENTS

FOREWORD

Guyana, the only English-speaking country of South America, is a very minor actor on the world stage, a rather isolated island, so to speak, on the northern shores of South America. Its population is under 1 million, and it has a gross national product less than half a billion dollars. It especially interests students of politics for a negative reason, because it is (like neighboring Surinam) such an outstanding failure story. It became independent in 1966 with good prospects, ample land and good natural resources, with a relatively educated population accustomed to British legal and political traditions. It has fallen into extreme poverty, with declining standards of health and education and an income level comparable to that of overcrowded and always despotic Haiti.

It has also sunk from functioning democracy to total dictatorship, under which the constitution frankly gives dictatorial powers to the president. Guyana is an unhappy example of the results of minority rule in a poor country. The party that managed to get power with majority support could not hold it without fraud and coercion; hence it engaged in ever more fraud and coercion and descended into the grossest tyranny. Absurd claims of socialism were used to give a veneer of idealism to narrow dictatorship, and irregular violence was indulged for no better reason than to instill fear.

Professor Singh, a native of Guyana and student of Caribbean politics, is in a good position to describe this melancholy development. Happily, he discerns reasons for hope in the latest turn of events, as the nation has been released by the death of Forbes Burnham; and the man who somewhat accidentally succeeded him, Desmond Hoyte, has turned his back on ideology. It is too soon to say whether a corner has been turned, and recovery cannot be swift, but Guyana may eventually prove that a country can not only sink irrationally into political disorder and social misery but recover sanity and well-being.

Robert Wesson
Series Editor

PREFACE

This book looks at the politics and government of Guyana after World War II. In large measure, it describes a political tragedy in that it examines how a liberal democracy succumbed to authoritarian tendencies resulting in a de facto one-party state. It shows how economic development became a casualty of over-centralization of political and economic decision making, and of a lack of public accountability on the part of the ruling elite. It raises questions about the adequacy of the central proposition of dependency theory that locates the cause of underdevelopment of ex-colonies like Guyana in their integration into the international capitalist economy. Certainly in the case of Guyana, the peculiar political superstructure and the role of the state in the economy, described in this book, must rank among the principal explanations for its underdevelopment.

I would like to acknowledge, with thanks, assistance received during the writing of this book. The following people helped by providing me with literature on Guyana: Lance Foldes, Laikhram Singh, Eusi Kwayana, Vishnu Bisram, A. Karshan, and Congressman Buddy Darden of Georgia's seventh congressional district. Berry College provided me with a library research grant to facilitate my use of the Caribbean collection at the University of Florida library. Deans Doyle Mathis and Barbara Abels of Berry College provided me with typing assistance, and Lucy Bredeson-Smith and Kathy Cromer uncomplainingly typed the various drafts of the manuscripts.

I owe a special debt of gratitude to Robert Wesson of the Hoover Institution for getting me started on this work and for his encouragement throughout the course of the manuscript preparation. I would also like to thank Bill Ratliff of the Hoover Institution for his extensive comments on an earlier draft of the manuscript. The recommendations of both Wesson and Ratliff guided the preparation of the final draft.

Finally, I would like to thank my wife, Kathy, for her patience and support throughout, but especially for singlehandedly taking care of our newborn son so as to release me to work on the book. As a token of my deep appreciation, this book is dedicated to her.

Chaitram Singh

ABBREVIATIONS

AIFLD   American Institute for Free Labor Development
ASCRIA   Association for Social and Cultural Relations with
               Independent Africa
BGEIA   British Guiana East Indian Association
BGLU   British Guiana Labor Union
CARICOM   Caribbean Common Market
CARIFTA   Caribbean Free Trade Association
CSA   Civil Service Association
CCWU   Clerical and Commercial Workers' Union
DEMBA   Demerara Bauxite Company
DLM   Democratic Labor Movement
GIWU   Guiana Industrial Workers' Union
GAWU   Guyana Agricultural Workers' Union
GBSA   Guyana Bauxite Supervisers' Union
GCC   Guyana Council of Churches
GCIO   Guyana Council of Indian Organizations
GDF   Guyana Defense Force
GLU   Guyana Labor Force
GUYMINE   Guyana Mining Enterprise
GMWU   Guyana Mine Workers' Union
GNS   Guyana National Service
GNTC   Guyana National Trading Corporation
GUYSUCO   Guyana Sugar Corporation
GTA   Guyana Teachers' Association

ORIT	Inter-American Regional Organization of Workers
ICFTU	International Confederation of Free Trade Unions
IPRA	Indian Political Revolutionary Associates
ITS	International Trade Secretariats
LCP	League of Colored Peoples
LP	Liberator Party
MPCA	Manpower Citizens' Association
NAACIE	National Association of Agricultural, Clerical, and Industrial Employees
NDF	National Democratic Front
NDP	National Democratic Party
NGS	National Guard Service
NLF	National Labor Front
PDM	People's Democratic Movement
PNC	People's National Congress
PPP	People's Progressive Party
PAC	Political Affairs Committee
PYO	Progressive Youth Organization
PSI	Public Service International Secretariat
PSU	Public Service Union
SSU	Special Service Unit
SPA	Sugar Producers' Association
TUC	Trades Union Congress (Trades Union Council until 1976)
UDP	United Democratic Party
UF	United Force
UGSA	University of Guyana Staff Association
VLD	Vanguard for Liberation and Democracy
WRSM	Women's Revolutionary Socialist Movement
WPA	Working People's Alliance
WPVP	Working People's Vanguard Party
WFTU	World Federation of Trade Unions
YSM	Youth Socialist Movement

1

THE LAND OF THE SIX RACES

INTRODUCTION

The Cooperative Republic of Guyana is the only one of its kind in the world. The title proclaims a socialist path of development centered around the cooperative. Formerly British Guiana, the country received its independence from Great Britain on May 26, 1966, at which time it underwent a name change.[1]

Guyanese society is very highly politicized. Most organizations are directly involved in the politics of the country. Governmental institutions, including the courts, which were very well respected during the colonial and early postcolonial years, have been reduced in stature by a party preoccupied with its own longevity in office. Although some of the formal trappings of a liberal democracy have been retained, the essential nature of the government is authoritarian. The ruling party maintains itself in power by electioneering malpractices and by the intimidation afforded by an elaborate military and para-military force.

Guyanese society in the 1980s is one gripped by fear. Violent crimes occur with great frequency and the police are unable or unwilling to apprehend the criminals. Shortages of food and medicine are common, and a great amount of productive time is spent queuing up in long lines for the limited supplies that are available. Many speak with nostalgia of the colonial days.[2] One suspects that it is not so much that these people want the British back as it is a way of dramatizing their present plight. Local politicians and outside commentators speak of the "Haitianization" of Guyana, a sad commentary on a country that used to boast of becoming the breadbasket of the British Caribbean.

The country seems to be living out an ideological fantasy. "Comrade" is the official form of salutation and socialist rhetoric is pervasive. North Korean-style mass games take place. Parks have been renamed "revolutionary squares" for revolutions that never occurred. Yet none of this hides the reality that in the 1980s, Guyana is an underdeveloped country whose economy has abscessed.

SITUATION

Guyana is situated on the northeastern shoulder of South America. It is the only English-speaking country on the continent. It occupies an area of 83,000 square miles or approximately the size of Great Britain. It is bounded on the west by Venezuela, on the east by Surinam, and on the south and southwest by Brazil. Its Atlantic coastline is about 270 miles long and stretches from Point Playa in the northwest to the Corentyne River in the east. The Corentyne River forms the boundary between Guyana and Surinam, and flows south to the Brazilian border. The country is traversed by numerous rivers flowing in a northerly direction. The three largest rivers—the Essequibo, the Demerara, and the Berbice rivers—give their names to the three counties that are the major subdivisions of the country. The capital of Guyana is Georgetown and is situated at the mouth of the Demerara River.

Guyana can be divided into four natural regions: the coastal plain, the hilly sand and clay belt, the highland region, and the interior savannahs.[3] Of these, the coastal plain is by far the most important and has dominated the history of the country. It is a narrow strip of land, varying in width from 10 to 40 miles, and running along the Atlantic shoreline from Point Playa in the northwest to the Corentyne River in the southeast. Much of the coastal plain is below sea level at high tide and has to be protected by an elaborate system of sea defenses. The silty clay soil on the coastal plain is very suitable for the cultivation of rice and sugar cane. Most of Guyana's population live on the coast. This is largely the result of the colonial settlement pattern and of the fact that this is climatically the most hospitable region in the country. The mean temperature at Georgetown is about 80 degrees Fahrenheit. Although the humidity is high, the constant breeze from the sea has a moderating effect.

The hilly sand and clay belt lies south of the coastal plain and covers about one-quarter of the country. The soil in this area is not suitable for farming. However, this region is rich in hardwood timbers, including greenheart, which Guyana exports. Guyana's bauxite deposits are also located in this area, around the towns of Linden, Ituni, and Kwakwani. The other major population center in this belt is Bartica which is a trading town and an important link between the capital and the interior of the country. There are also some Amerindian reservations in this area.

In the southwestern corner of the country is the Rupununi Savannah occupying an area of about 6,000 square miles. The Rupununi Savannah and the smaller Ebini Savannah located on the Berbice River provide most of the cattle grazing in the country. The rest of the country is mountainous and very sparsely populated. Dense forests, heavy rainfall, and numerous rivers make overland transportation difficult. These conditions, combined with poor communications with the capital, make the highland region unattractive to settlers. The highland region is very rich in mineral resources. Some of the largest gold and diamond fields in Guyana are located here. That this region has remained underdeveloped is due to the fact that it is at the center of a border dispute between Venezuela and Guyana.

Guyana has been called "the land of the six races," because of its racial composition. The ethnic categories are East Indians, blacks, Amerindians, Chinese, Mixed Races, Portuguese,[4] and other Europeans. The population of Guyana is approximately 788,000 people, of which Indians and blacks make up the overwhelming majority. The Indians account for 51 percent, blacks 31 percent, Mixed Races 12 percent, Amerindians 4 percent, and Chinese and Europeans 2 percent.[5] The annual rate of population increase over the last decade has been less than 1 percent. This is because the natural increase based on births and deaths is more than halved by out-migration.[6]

EARLY COLONIAL HISTORY

Guyana was the first territory in the New World to be explored by non-Iberians. What is today Guyana was originally three separate Dutch colonies: Essequibo, Demerara, and Berbice. Around 1616, a Dutch trading post was established on the Essequibo coast in the northwest. The Dutch West India company eventually acquired control over this trading post. It was under the aegis of this company that the colony of Berbice was established further to the southeast. The Demerara colony, which was located between Essequibo and Berbice, developed much later as an appendage to Essequibo.[7]

The colonies changed hands several times before they finally came under effective British control. The British first took possession of these colonies from the Dutch in 1781. However, during the following year, the French, who were at war with Britain, captured these territories. At the peace settlement in 1783, the colonies were returned to the Dutch. In 1796, the British captured the colonies again and maintained control over them for six years. By the Treaty of Amiens in 1802, the Dutch regained possession of the territories. However, war broke out between the Netherlands and Great Britain in 1803, and the British recaptured all three of these Dutch colonies. Finally, in 1814, the Netherlands formally ceded Essequibo, Demerara, and Berbice to Great Britain. In 1831, the three colonies were united to form the colony of British Guiana, with the administrative center at Georgetown.[8] The colony remained under British rule until 1966 when it was granted its independence and renamed Guyana.

Despite the frequent changes in the ownership of the colonies, there was continuity both in the way the colony was administered and in the way society was organized. The British initially adopted the system of administration that had been put in place by the Dutch.[9] However, what provided enduring continuity in the life of the colony was the way agricultural production was organized. The Dutch had introduced the plantation system of agriculture into Guyana, and the British continued it. The plantations played a central role in the colonization of Guyana. Immigration into the colony responded to the labor needs of the plantations, and the social structure of the colony reflected the organization of work on the plantations. The plantations were, without a doubt, the hub of life in the colony.

THE EMERGENCE OF THE SUGAR MONOCULTURE

Although the pursuit of trading opportunities initially brought the Dutch to Guyana, sugar production eventually became their primary interest. The European demand for sugar exceeded the capability of the Spanish colonies to supply this commodity. The Dutch therefore saw the introduction of sugar cane into Guyana as a profitable undertaking.

In 1658, the Dutch began their sugar cane cultivation with slave labor on the Pomeroon River. However, war between the Netherlands and Great Britain resulted in the disbanding of this settlement. The Dutch later set up sugar plantations in the Essequibo colony where they utilized the slash-and-burn method of cultivation. Repeated cultivation in a particular area led to soil depletion and deteriorating crop yields, and new clearings became necessary. Under these conditions, sugar exports were small and financial losses were enormous. Several sugar plantations were abandoned as worthless. The new ones that were established followed the same fate.[10] As a result, large-scale sugar cane cultivation never took root in Essequibo.

The period 1742–1772 was probably the most important period of the Dutch rule. During this period, Laurens Storm Van's Gravesande served as the governor of Essequibo. In 1746, Gravesande opened up the Demerara region to settlement, inaugurating what Adamson calls "the littoral phase of Guyana's history."[11] Gravesande's new policy resulted in the immigration of British settlers from the Caribbean islands and in the transfer of British capital and British slave labor to Demerara. Guyana was attractive to these settlers because the soil in the Caribbean islands had begun to wear out, and the new settlers believed that the soil in Guyana was so rich that little more was required than to plant the sugar cane in the rainy season and to reap it in the dry season. They also believed that the cost of maintaining their slaves would be low since provisions for the consumption of the slaves could be grown in Guyana. The new settlers saw some additional advantages. In the Caribbean islands, removal of the sugar cane from the field was done by mules. This was very expensive and cut into the profits of the owners. By contrast, the land in Guyana was flat, and cheap transportation by water was possible. Finally, Guyana was outside of the path of hurricanes and its climate was assessed to be mild and wholesome.[12]

At first, cultivation on the coast was avoided because it was almost entirely covered by swamps, but also because it was exposed to the exploits of French and English pirates. The sugar estates were initially laid out on the banks of the Demerara River. These eventually failed because of soil depletion. Sugar production in Guyana began on a large scale when the swampy coastal plain was finally brought under irrigation through a system of polders introduced by the Dutch and continued by the British. However, the soil in the freshly reclaimed area contained a great amount of salt and was more suited for cotton than for sugar cultivation. It was only after continual rain washing and the exclusion of further contamination from the sea water that the soil eventually became right for sugar cane.[13] Not surprisingly, cotton was for a while the principal export of both Demerara and Berbice, where the system of polders had been employed. In fact, for a short period at the end of the eighteenth century, Guyana was the largest cotton producer in the world. However, Guyana could not compete with the southern states of the United States, and the effect of that competition was felt as early as 1802. Besides, the British abolished the slave trade in 1807 and further increase in Guyana's cotton cultivation became very difficult.[14]

In both Berbice and Demerara, plantations that were sheltered from strong winds cultivated coffee as one of their staple products. Although Guyana was a major coffee producer, the Napoleonic continental system and the refusal of the British government to allow West Indian producers to export to the United States adversely affected the future of Guyanese coffee production. Also, Ceylon, with cheap and plentiful labor, was emerging as the chief coffee producer in the British Empire, and Guyana could not compete. After 1810, coffee and cotton output in Guyana began to decline. Coffee and cotton plantations were being converted to sugar. With the collapse of cotton and coffee, sugar became the dominant staple in the economy of the colony.[15]

"BOOKERS' GUIANA"

Several developments in the sugar economy led to amalgamation and concentration in Guyana's sugar industry. Guyana's sugar, like that of the other British Caribbean territories, entered Great Britain under a preferential duty system. This position of privilege was threatened in the 1820s by changes in imperial commercial policy. In 1825, sugar from Mauritius began to enter the British market on equal terms with sugar from Guyana and the other British Caribbean territories. In 1836, the duties of the sugar from both the Caribbean and from India were equalized, thereby forcing the British Caribbean to compete with the cheapest free labor supply in the world.[16] However, the event that caused dramatic changes in the sugar industry in Guyana was the emancipation of the slaves in 1838. Fears arising from emancipation set in motion "a change of ownership so extensive as to constitute a revolution in itself."[17] At the time of emancipation, there were 308 sugar estates in cultivation in Guyana. Between 1838 and 1853, 175 sugar estates changed owners, and over the same period of time 135 sugar estates were abandoned. Reductions in the number of sugar estates continued through the end of the nineteenth century. Largely as a result of amalgamations, the number of sugar plantations fell from 173 in 1853 to 105 in 1884. The collapse of sugar prices in 1884 and in 1894 caused many additional failures. By 1904, the number of operating sugar plantations had fallen to 46.[18]

Two companies—Booker Brothers and John McConnell and Company—managed to avoid the financial difficulties experienced by the major companies. During the 1860s and 1870s, Booker Brothers and John McConnell and Company had concentrated on the mercantile aspects of sugar, instead of sugar estate ownership. They were able to exploit the difficulties of the post–1884 crisis and to establish themselves in a commanding position in the industry. In 1900, Booker Brothers and John McConnell and Company amalgamated to become the corporate entity, Booker Brothers McConnell and Company Limited.[19] The company was able to extend itself to the point where it exercised a virtual monopoly over the sugar industry. In 1967, it controlled 15 of Guyana's 18 sugar plantations.

However, the influence of Bookers, as the company was commonly called, was not limited to the sugar industry. It was involved in almost every other sector of the Guyanese economy. It managed a network of wholesale and retail stores, dealing in a vast assortment of commodities from groceries to automobiles. Bookers operated the largest taxi service in Guyana. It was involved in the manufacture and sale of drugs, medical supplies, and boxes. It produced and distributed rum, stockfeed, balata, lumber, and petroleum products. The company was also involved in publishing, advertising, real estate, insurance, and in cattle ranching. Bookers even had its own shipping service.[20]

Bookers enjoyed very high visibility in the economy of the country. Bookers was to Guyana what the United Fruit Company was to Guatemala. Indeed, because it appeared as though Bookers literally owned the country, it was common to hear Guyanese refer to the colony as "Bookers' Guiana" instead of British Guiana. The power and influence of Bookers spilled into the political sphere, and Bookers became symbolic of British rule over the colony. But to the Africans and Indians in Guyana, Bookers evoked a more intense visceral feeling. To the Africans, the operations of Bookers recalled ancestral miseries suffered on the plantations, while to the Indians, Bookers represented all of the degradations of plantation life, some of which continued into the 1960s. It is therefore easy to understand why after World War II, nationalist politicians found that attacking Bookers was a useful strategy for political mobilization.

THE PLANTATION NEXUS

Slavery

The primary interest of both the Dutch and the British in Guyana was sugar. Until emancipation in 1838, labor on the sugar plantations was provided by African slaves. The importation of slaves into the colony began in the early 1620s and continued up until the beginning of the nineteenth century. At the time of emancipation, there were about 84,915 slaves in Guyana.[21]

The conditions of life to which the slaves were subjected were harsh and degrading, though the harshness of treatment apparently varied from plantation to plantation. According to one account, the slaves lived in quarters made of frail materials plastered with mud. They had no fireplaces or chimneys, and rarely did these accommodations have windows. The slaves were not permitted to have any furniture and their domestic possessions were limited to an iron pot per slave family and a blanket for each person to sleep on. The slaves subsisted primarily on plantains and ground provisions which they themselves grew. Salted codfish was imported for the consumption of the slaves, but the supplies were often putrid on arrival. Every possible way was devised to keep the slaves dependent on the plantation, and since a literate slave was perceived to be a threat to the plantation, the slaves were kept illiterate.[22]

Slave rebellions were frequent in Guyana but they were usually brutally repressed. The most famous Guyanese slave rebellion occurred in February 1763 when the slaves, led by Cuffy, controlled the greater part of the colony of Berbice for 11 months. The Dutch were able to reestablish control with the aid of troop reinforcements from Holland. Cuffy took his own life, but the surviving rebel leaders were reputedly roasted alive over a slow flame.[23] Cuffy has been elevated to the status of Guyana's national hero and a statue of him now stands outside of the president's residence.

Slavery ended when capitalist interest in free labor dovetailed with the humanitarian movement against slavery and resulted in the Emancipation Act of 1834. The act required a period of apprenticeship of six years for the field slaves and four years for all other slaves. The slave owners of Guyana were compensated for the loss of unpaid slave capital at an average rate of 51 pounds sterling per slave. The slaves, on the other hand, had to be content with their freedom since, lamentably, "It occurred to no one to compensate the slaves for their previous bondage."[24]

The exslaves tried to acquire their own land in order to support themselves and maintain their independence from the plantations. Large groups of exslaves pooled their money and bought abandoned plantations, which were then subdivided among the proprietors. They encountered serious drainage problems that they were never successful in overcoming. After 1852, it became evident that the former slaves had not become an independent peasantry but depended heavily on wages from the plantations. The majority gave up any idea of owning their own land or setting up their own business. Many migrated to the towns and became wage earners. Those villagers with some education took up elementary schoolteaching. The civil service provided another avenue for advancement. The civil service had grown in size and many lower grade clerical positions became available to locals. Blacks with some education entered at this level.[25] Large numbers of blacks also began to enter the lower ranks of the police force. Many became "pork-knockers," itinerant prospectors for gold and diamonds in the interior of the country. In 1914, bauxite mining operations began up the Demerara River. This attracted many blacks. After World War II, the scale of mining operations increased and set in motion large-scale black migration to the bauxite mining towns of Linden and Kwakwani.

Since independence in 1966, blacks have dominated certain areas of activity. Blacks dominate the civil service, the postal service, the army, the police force, and dockworkers. The paramilitary National Service, established in 1973, is predominantly black, as is the People's Militia, created in 1976. The work force in the state-owned bauxite industry and in the state-owned segment of the banking industry is almost completely black. Blacks own most of the nightclubs. They are very prominent in the teaching profession though the majority of Guyana's teachers are Indians. The bureaucracy of the ruling party has expanded enormously, providing jobs primarily to blacks. The government has tried to interest blacks in agriculture, but its efforts have not met with any measurable degree of success.

The Indenture System

The movement of the Africans into the villages and towns after emancipation created a serious labor shortage on the sugar plantations. In order to assure themselves of a large supply of cheap labor, the plantation owners introduced a system of indentured labor. Laborers who were induced to go to Guyana under the indenture system were generally required to serve a five-year term, after which they could remain in Guyana or return home with their savings. The life of the indentured laborer differed very little from that of the African slaves who had preceded him on the plantation. The major difference, of course, was that the indentured laborer was mentally free and could look forward to leaving the plantation at the end of the indentured term.

Between 1835 and 1839, small numbers of English, Irish, and Germans were imported into Guyana as contract laborers. Many became victims of tropical diseases or excessive drinking. Others abandoned the plantation for more profitable occupations. However, three groups of indentured laborers made a tremendous impact on the development of the colony. These were the Portuguese, the Chinese, and the Indians. Between 1835 and 1862, 31,628 Portuguese laborers were imported into Guyana under the indenture system. At the end of their indenture, they moved into the relatively underdeveloped retail trade and in a very short time completely dominated this economic sector. Between 1853 and 1912, approximately 14,000 Chinese laborers came to Guyana. After their indenture terms ended, they also moved into retail trades. They intermarried with members of the other ethnic groups and became very assimilated into Guyanese society. The largest number of indentured laborers were brought from India. Between 1838 and 1917, the year that the indenture system ended, 238,960 Indians came to Guyana.[26] They became the backbone of the labor force on the sugar plantations.

The indentured Indians lived in relative isolation from the other ethnic groups. Their living and working conditions approximated that of the slaves before them. They were housed in the old slave "logies" or in congested barrack blocks. Their isolation from the other ethnic groups was accentuated by their cultural distinctiveness. The plantation owners encouraged the continuation of the Indian culture and even built temples and mosques to allow the Hindus and the Moslems to practice their respective religions.[27]

Like the other indentured laborers before them, the Indians were also anxious to leave the plantations. There were two patterns of departure from the plantations. The first took the form of repatriation to India. It is estimated that, between 1843 and 1949, about 75,547 Indians returned to India as part of the official repatriation scheme. The second pattern involved resettlement in other parts of Guyana and the establishment of an independent peasantry. The majority of those who left the plantations were encouraged by the availability of cheap land to remain in Guyana and become farmers.[28] Despite these departures, a large number of Indians remained on the sugar plantations.

Guyana's rice industry was developed almost entirely by the Indians who chose to make Guyana their home. They began rice cultivation in earnest in Guyana around 1893. By 1917, Guyana was self-sufficient in rice and, shortly afterwards, rice became one of its exports.[29] The prosperity from rice allowed the Indians to acquire more land and, by 1950, the Indians had consolidated their position in agriculture. Success in the rice industry also allowed the Indians to venture into the retail business which they now dominate. Prosperity from agriculture and business aided the preparation of the younger generation for the professions. The result is that Indians dominate the medical and legal professions, and account for the majority of the teachers in the country.

NOTES

1. The name Guyana will be used throughout the monograph, even when reference is made to the colonial period.

2. The author visited Guyana in June 1985 and spoke with sugar workers and rice farmers in the Corentyne area.

3. For an elaboration on the geography of Guyana, see Leslie P. Cummings, *Geography of Guyana* (London: Collins, 1976).

4. British colonial authorities maintained a separate ethnic category for the Portuguese. This practice was continued after independence.

5. The most recent census was conducted in 1980. However, the results have not yet been made public.

6. The World Bank, *Guyana: A Framework for Economic Recovery* (Washington, D.C.: The World Bank, 1985), p. 80.

7. James Rodway, *Guiana: British, Dutch and French* (London: T. Fisher Urwin, 1912), pp. 47–88, 250.

8. Raymond T. Smith, *British Guiana* (London: Oxford University Press, 1962), pp. 11–26.

9. *Ibid.*, pp. 20–25.

10. Rodway, *Guiana*, pp. 250–252. See also Smith, *British Guiana*, p. 15.

11. Alan Adamson, *Sugar Without Slaves* (New Haven: Yale University Press, 1972), p. 20.

12. *Ibid.*, p. 21.

13. Rodway, *Guiana*, pp. 253–255.

14. Adamson, *Sugar Without Slaves*, p. 25.

15. *Ibid.*, pp. 25–26. See also Rodway, *Guiana*, p. 256.

16. Adamson, *Sugar Without Slaves*, p. 26.

17. *Ibid.*, p. 160.

18. *Ibid.*, pp. 160–161, 209. See also R. W. Beachey, *The British West Indies Sugar Industry in the Late 19th Century* (Oxford: Basil Blackwell, 1957), pp. 118–119

19. Adamson, *Sugar Without Slaves*, pp. 211–212.

20. Leo A. Despres, *Cultural Pluralism and Nationalist Politics in British Guiana* (Chicago: Rand McNally and Company, 1967), pp. 137–141.

21. Smith, *British Guiana*, p. 38.

22. Peter Simms, *Trouble in Guyana* (London: George Allen & Urwin Ltd., 1966), pp. 39–41.

23. Smith, *British Guiana*, p. 19. See also Robert H. Manley, *Guyana Emergent: The Post-Independence Struggle for Nondependent Development* (Cambridge, Mass.: Shenkman Publishing Company, Inc., 1982), p. 3.

24. Adamson, *Sugar Without Slaves*, p. 31.

25. Smith, *British Guiana*, pp. 39–43. See also Simms, *Trouble in Guyana*. pp. 45–48.

26. Smith, *British Guiana*. pp. 42–46. For a more extensive historical treatment of indentured immigration to Guyana, see Dwarka Nath, *A History of Indians in Guyana* (London: Butler & Tanner Ltd., 1970).

27. Smith, *British Guiana*, pp. 46–48.

28. *Ibid.*, pp. 49–5l.

29. Nath, *A History of Indians*, pp. 110–111.

2

THE DIFFICULT PATH TO INDEPENDENCE

INTRODUCTION

The struggle for Guyana's independence began after World War II. After the war, British Caribbean territories anticipated major changes in colonial policies. The ideas expressed in the Atlantic Charter, particularly regarding the question of national self-determination, impressed intellectuals in the Caribbean. West Indians, including Guyanese, who had served with the British in the war, returned home with altered expectations. At a minimum, they hoped for political equality with the British. The independence movements in other parts of the British Empire, notably in India and Ghana, captured the imagination of indigenous leaders in the British Caribbean. The goal of independence for the British Caribbean territories was also encouraged by the British government which hoped that the territories would form a federation within the British Commonwealth.

In Guyana, the independence movement began as a coalition between the two major ethnic groups, the East Indians and the blacks. However, the movement became torn by ideological differences, leadership disputes, and ethnic antagonism. The divisions provided an opening for foreign intervention that further aggravated these divisions, and in the early 1960s, Guyana convulsed under civil strife. When independence came in 1966, Guyana was a racially divided society and the prospect of national integration appeared as elusive as ever.

THE POWER STRUCTURE AT THE END OF WORLD WAR II

Mass political mobilization did not begin in Guyana until the establishment of the People's Progressive Party (PPP) in 1950. However, there were ethnic organizations that attempted to advance the interests of the different ethnic groups. The two largest ethnic organizations were the League of Colored Peoples (LCP), which claimed to represent the interests of blacks in the colony, and the British Guiana East Indian Association (BGEIA), which claimed to represent the Indians. Both of these organizations were controlled by middle class elements and their impact on the system was primarily at the cultural level. The Chinese Association and the Sword of the Spirit performed the same functions for the Chinese and Portuguese respectively.

The constitution in effect in the colony after World War II did not provide for the administration of the colony by elected officials. Rather, the colony was administered by the Executive Council, consisting of the governor and other appointed officials. The Executive Council was assisted by the Legislative Council, an unrepresentative body made up of 30 members, only 14 of whom were elected and then only on the basis of a franchise limited by literacy and property qualifications. The governor and his principal assistants, the colonial secretary and the attorney general, were ex officio members of the Legislative Council. The other members of the Legislative Council were nominated by the governor, eight official members and five nonofficial members.[1] The constitution also provided that "any matter requiring a vote or enactment of the Legislative Council may be decided by the Governor according to his own deliberative judgement notwithstanding that such decision may be contrary to the vote of the majority of the Council."[2] Democracy was certainly not a concern of this constitution. Indeed, the idea of government deriving its powers from the consent of the governed was still heresy in the colonial context.

The political system was an exclusionary one. Since there was no provision for any elected group of persons taking office, political parties were not encouraged. Ethnic organizations such as the LCP and the BGEIA were tolerated because they did not fundamentally threaten the power structure. In the scheme of things, the governor functioned like a constitutional dictator. His administration was wedded to the interests of the sugar companies. This was evident from the appointments he made on the Executive Council and his nominations to the Legislative Council. It was also evident in the willingness of the colonial administration to use force to put down protests by workers over wages and working conditions. In this latter regard, a familiar pattern developed. As Hugh Tinker has put it: "The workers would protest; the police would be summoned to put down the tumult; there would be firings, deaths, a commission of enquiry; recommendations, silence—until the next incident."[3] Nevertheless, the first major challenge to the system came from combinations of workers.

The first trade union to be established in Guyana was the British Guiana Labor Union (BGLU), launched in 1919 by Hubert N. Critchlow, who is regarded as the father of trade unionism in Guyana. Critchlow had been active in the waterfront workers' strikes in Georgetown since

1905. In 1918, he began organizing a union after he was fired from his job for circulating a petition calling for an eight-hour work day. By the end of 1919, the BGLU had about 7,000 members. It was registered as Guyana's first trade union in 1922, one year after the British government, reflecting domestic opinion in Britain, instructed its administrative officials in Guyana to enact the Trades Union Ordinance.[4]

There was a flood of trade union registrations in the late 1930s.[5] Between November 1937 and October 1938, seven trade unions were registered. The most important of these was the Manpower Citizens' Association (MPCA). The union was launched by Ayube Edun who, by his writings, had established himself as a champion of the sugar workers. The MPCA set about organizing the sugar workers, especially the field laborers, and the response to the union was overwhelming. However, despite the growing strength of the union, the Sugar Producers' Association (SPA) refused to recognize the MPCA as the bargaining agent of the sugar workers.[6] The workers then turned to strike action to force the issue. On February 13, 1939, the sugar workers at Plantation Leonora went on strike and demanded that management negotiate with the MPCA. On February 16, the striking workers became threatening. MPCA leaders refused to go to the sugar estate to pacify the workers unless the union was granted full recognition. The management refused to grant recognition to the MPCA and instead brought in armed policemen. There were several clashes between the police and the strikers. Finally, the police opened fire on the strikers, killing four people and wounding several others. A commission of inquiry was instituted to report on the circumstances surrounding the disturbances at Leonora and neighboring areas. However, before the conclusion of the inquiry in March, the SPA agreed to recognize the MPCA as the sole bargaining agent of the sugar workers.[7]

The MPCA leadership played a very significant role in the Guyanese labor movement until 1976 when it was replaced by a rival sugar union. After its recognition in 1939, it continued to increase in size and by 1943, its membership exceeded 20,000, making it the largest union in the colony.[8] Because of its size, the MPCA was able to exert considerable influence on the Trades Union Council (TUC), the umbrella organization of organized labor in Guyana. However, in the 1950s and 1960s, that influence tended to be of a reactionary nature.

THE ESTABLISHMENT OF THE PEOPLE'S PROGRESSIVE PARTY

The People's Progressive Party is generally regarded as the party that Cheddi Jagan built. It was the first mass-based party in Guyana. Jagan was one of its founders and has been its only leader. There is no question of the great impact this man and this party have had on Guyanese politics.

Cheddi B. Jagan was born and raised in Port Mourant, a sugar plantation where his parents were laborers. He received his secondary education at Queen's College, one of Guyana's finest secondary schools. In 1936, he entered Howard University in the United States on a two-year predental course, after which he transferred to Northwestern University to continue his training in dentistry. In 1942, he graduated from the Northwestern University Dental School.[9]

Life on a sugar plantation had made an indelible impression on Jagan's mind. As he later wrote,

The plantation appeared to me as the hub of life. Everything revolved around sugar, and the sugar planters seemed to own the world. . . . The plantation was indeed a world of its own. Or rather it was two worlds: the world of exploiters and the world of the exploited; the world of whites and the world of non-whites. One was the world of managers and the European staff in their splendid mansions; the other the world of the labourers in their logies in the "niggeryard" and the "bound-coolie-yard." The mansions were electrically lit; the logies had kerosene lamps. It was not unusual to hear that mules were better treated than human beings, for the stables had electric light. It was not that electricity could not have been taken to the workers' quarters and residences. The owners could easily have generated more electricity at very little extra cost to satisfy the needs of all. But electricity, like so many other things, was a status symbol.[10]

Reaction to the injustices of life in plantation Guyana motivated Jagan's interest in political affairs. While at Northwestern University, he took courses in the social sciences at the YMCA College in Chicago. His interest in political affairs was encouraged and guided by Professor Sinha, an exile from India who taught at the college. Whatever other influences there may have been on Jagan, and he acknowledges several,[11] none proved to be deeper and more enduring than Marxist writings. Both Cheddi Jagan and Janet Rosenberg, whom he met in Chicago and married before returning to Guyana in 1943, accepted the principles of Marxism-Leninism and proceeded to apply that body of doctrine to the Guyana situation.

Cheddi Jagan entered public life in Guyana in 1945 as the treasurer of the sugar union, the MPCA. After a year with the union, Jagan was removed from his office as treasurer by the union hierarchy. Jagan claims that this was the punishment meted out to him by the union leadership because he had objected to the high expense allowances of union officials and to the tendency of union leaders to collaborate with the owners of the sugar plantations.[12] Jagan reacted by actively supporting Dr. J. P. Latchmansingh, president of the BGEIA, who was trying to set up a rival union in the sugar industry. The new union, which was called the

Guiana Industrial Workers' Union (GIWU), became involved in a protracted struggle with the MPCA for recognition as the sole bargaining agent for the sugar workers.[13]

Both Jagan and his wife were members of a group that discussed public policy issues at the Carnegie Library in Georgetown. However, they felt that a formal political organization was necessary if they were to make a greater impact. In 1946, they got together with Ashton Chase, a young black trade unionist, and Jocelyn Hubbard, a white Marxist who was the general secretary of the Trades Union Council, and formed a political group called the Political Affairs Committee (PAC).[14] The organization published a bulletin as part of its program of political education. On the masthead of the bulletin, PAC pledged "to assist the growth and development of the Labour and Progressive Movements of British Guiana, to the end of establishing a strong, disciplined and enlightened Party, equipped with the theory of Scientific Socialism."[15] Within a year, PAC faced its first electoral contest.

The November 1947 elections were the first elections held in Guyana since World War II. The elections were based on a limited franchise. Three members of PAC, Cheddi Jagan, Janet Jagan, and Jocelyn Hubbard, contested the elections as independents. Of the three, only Cheddi Jagan won a seat in the Legislative Council, which he assumed in December.[16] Jagan used his parliamentary status to assail the privileged position of the sugar producers, and at street corner meetings, he gave a running account of the legislative proceedings. While his impact on the sugar producers was negligible, he did develop a large following among working class Guyanese.

The event that catapulted the Jagans to even greater prominence was the killing of five sugar workers by the police during a strike in 1948. The strike stemmed from sugar workers' dissatisfaction with a change in the system of cutting sugar cane and loading it into the punts. The system that was supplanted treated the cutting of the sugar cane as one operation and the loading of the sugar cane into punts as another. They were performed by two different groups of workers. The change that was introduced required that cane cutters should also do the loading. The workers complained that it was tiring to switch from the task of cutting the cane to the other of picking it up and carrying it from the field to the punts. They argued that there were frequently not sufficient punts available and that the cane cutters' time was wasted when they had to wait for one to arrive. The workers also complained that the planks leading up to the punts were narrow and slippery and were particularly dangerous for the older men who could otherwise cope with the task of cutting cane.[17] These complaints had been expressed to the recognized sugar union, the MPCA. However, the MPCA negotiated with the Sugar Producers' Association, not on the demand of reverting to the established system of regarding cutting and loading as two separate operations as the sugar workers desired, but on the price to be paid to the workers under the new system. Under the agreement reached between the MPCA and the SPA, the workers would receive a marginal increase in the price per ton of sugar cane cut and loaded.[18]

The workers were not satisfied with the MPCA-SPA agreement and on April 17, 1948, the workers went on strike on the following eight sugar estates on the east coast of Demerara: Ogle, Industry, Vryheid's Lust, Mon Repos, La Bonne Intention, Lusignan, Non Pareil, and Enmore. The MPCA tried to get the workers to resume work while the newly formed Guiana Industrial Workers' Union accused the MPCA of betraying the workers and urged the workers to remain on strike. The strike developed into a recognition struggle for the GIWU and received the active support of the Political Affairs Committee. Both Cheddi and Janet Jagan were actively involved in directing the strike. The Jagans addressed several meetings of the strikers and encouraged them to maintain their unity in the struggle for their rights. The Jagans also attended to the day-to-day organization of the strike. They were involved in raising money for the strikers, in organizing soup kitchens, and also in propaganda work. The Political Affairs Committee published agitational bulletins that were widely circulated at the GIWU meetings.[19]

The strike ended on June 16 when the police opened fire on a large group of demonstrators at the rear of the sugar factory at Plantation Enmore. The policemen were apparently concerned about the safety of the factory and about their own physical safety. Five Indian sugar workers were killed and 14 others wounded. A commission of inquiry found that several of the workers had been shot in the back while attempting to flee the police.[20]

The Jagans used the Enmore incident to publicize the deplorable conditions on the sugar plantations and to present the GIWU as the true union of the sugar workers. They organized a 16-mile funeral march from Enmore to Georgetown. The march was joined by thousands of sugar workers. Although the GIWU did not win the recognition of the Sugar Producers' Association, the entire affair boosted the image of the Jagans considerably. In the words of Janet Jagan, "Enmore made us."[21]

The upsurge in popularity of its leaders suggested to the Political Affairs Committee the propitiousness of establishing a mass-based political party. The move was recommended by considerations with regard to the future political development of the colony. There was every indication that the colony's constitution would be liberalized to permit internal self-government. In 1947, the British Secretary of State for the Colonies had convened a conference in Jamaica to consider proposals for a possible federation of the British Caribbean territories.[22] Guyana was represented at that conference. The future status of the colony seemed to be either as an independent nation or as part of an independent West Indian Federation. In either case, mass political parties would be crucial for the future governing of Guyana.

The Political Affairs Committee became worried that, as currently constituted, it might not be able to win the support of the majority of the Indians and Africans in the colony. While the majority of the Indians were captivated by Cheddi Jagan's leadership, the PAC leadership was concerned that the same could not be said of the majority of the Africans. The search began for a prestigious black person whose presence within the leadership of the new party would assure the organization of the eventual support of the majority of the Afro-Guyanese. The choice fell on Forbes Burnham, a brilliant young lawyer who had recently returned from his studies in Britain.

Linden Forbes Sampson Burnham, who later dominated Guyanese politics, was born in Kitty, a suburb of Georgetown, where his father was the headmaster of a primary school. He received his secondary education at Central High School and at Queen's College. In 1942 he won the Guiana Scholarship which was awarded annually by the government to the top student in the colony to enable the recipient to obtain a university education in Britain. However, because of the war, Burnham did not go immediately to Britain. Instead, he completed a bachelor's degree externally and taught first at a private secondary school and later at Queen's College. In 1945, he went to Britain to study law. His skill as an orator won him the Best Speaker's Cup of the Laws Faculty. While in Britain, he served as the president of the West Indian Students' Union and led the West Indian Students' Delegation to the World Youth Festival in Czechoslovakia. He is known to have had ties with the left-wing of the British Labour Party and also with the British Communist Party. In 1947, he received his law degree with honors, and the following year, he was called to the bar at Gray's Inn. In 1949, Burnham returned to Guyana and set up a private practice in law.[23]

Burnham joined forces with Jagan and the other PAC leaders and, in January 1950, they launched a new party which, following the suggestion of the British Communist Party, they named the People's Progressive Party (PPP).[24] Cheddi Jagan was to be the party leader. The other key executive positions were assigned as follows: Forbes Burnham was made chairman of the party; Clinton Wong, a Chinese, became senior vice-chairman; Cheddi Jagan was also second vice-chairman; Rory Westmaas, an Afro-Guyanese, was made junior vice-chairman; Ram Karran, an Indian, was the party treasurer; Janet Jagan was the party general secretary; and Sydney King, an Afro-Guyanese, was made assistant secretary.[25] The party proclaimed its purpose as follows:

The People's Progressive Party, recognizing that the final abolition of exploitation and oppression, of economic crises and unemployment and war will be achieved only by the Socialist organization of society, pledges itself to the task of winning a free and independent Guiana, of building a just socialist society, in which the industries of the country shall be socially and democratically owned and managed for the common good, a society in which security, plenty, peace, and freedom shall be the heritage of all.[26]

The PPP started out with no serious political competitors. The multiracial composition of its leadership and the goal of political independence from Great Britain gave it national appeal. However, almost from the beginning, two factions crystallized from differences over strategy. One faction headed by the Jagans was extremely ideological and dedicated to the struggle against capitalism and colonialism everywhere. It maintained extensive contacts within the world communist movement and took a keen interest in the affairs of other colonies. The party weekly newspaper, *Thunder*, under the editorship of Mrs. Jagan, frequently printed articles sent out by the British *Daily Worker* and by the British Communist Party, which was acting as the ideological mentor of the PPP. The Jagans imported and dispensed literature on Marxism and on the achievements of communist countries. The Jagans, as well as others within the party, participated in the conferences, congresses and rallies of communist and left-wing organizations in Europe.[27]

The other faction within the party, which was headed by Forbes Burnham, was critical of the party's involvements overseas and of its pronouncements on international affairs. This faction seemed to be much more sensitive to the state of international tension existing at the time. It was also worried about the wave of anticommunist hysteria that was sweeping through the United States in the early 1950s and about the impact this might have on Guyana. This faction argued that the party's persistence in procommunist activities could be used as an excuse to proscribe the party or to deny the colony its independence. However, despite the differences between the two factions, the party held together.[28]

In October 1951, a new constitution for Guyana was promulgated. The changes incorporated into the new constitution were the result of a commission of inquiry headed by Dr. E. J. Waddington. The Waddington Commission came to Guyana in December 1950 to investigate the political structure and economic capabilities of the colony and to make recommendations on the question of putting the colony on the path to self-government. The key provisions of the Waddington Constitution were:

1. universal adult suffrage, with no income qualifications for those running for election;
2. a bicameral legislature with a life of four years, comprising a House of As-

sembly as a lower house of twenty-four elected members and three ex officio members (the chief secretary, the attorney general and the financial secretary); and a State Council as an upper house of nine members, six appointed by the governor and two appointed by the majority group holding office, and one by the opposition;

3. the principal governing body would be the Executive Council with the governor as president, the three ex officio members of the House of Assembly, six ministers chosen by ballot from among the elected members of the House of Assembly, and a member of the State Council elected by that body to be minister without portfolio.

Although the constitution fell short of what the PPP had expected, the party still regarded it as one of the most advanced colonial constitutional instruments of that period.[29] For the first time in the colony's history, provisions existed for a group of elected ministers to conduct the internal affairs of the colony, subject only to the veto powers of the governor. Elections under this constitution were scheduled for April 27, 1953.

The principal opposition to the PPP came from the National Democratic Party (NDP). The NDP was formed in 1951 by two lawyers, John Carter, an Afro-Guyanese, and Lionel Luckhoo, an Indian, who was also president of the MPCA. The rest of the party consisted of a few Portuguese and African businessmen, members of the League of Colored Peoples, and other officials of the MPCA. There was a clear attempt to portray the party as an amalgam of the principal ethnic groups of the colony. In terms of ideology, the NDP was militantly anticommunist and saw the socialist PPP as an anathema to the future development of Guyana. In 1952, when Lionel Luckhoo was a nominated member of the Legislative Council, he authored the Undesirable Publications Act that allowed the governor to prevent the entry of any literature deemed to be "subversive and contrary to the public interest."[30] The legislation was aimed at the PPP, which imported communist literature for sale and distribution in the colony. However, as Peter Simms pointed out, "Mr. Luckhoo's proposal did for Communist literature what the case against Penguin Books later achieved for *Lady Chatterley's Lover*."[31]

The NDP was no match for the PPP, and this became clear in the April 1953 elections. Despite an intense anticommunist campaign by the NDP, it suffered an ignominious defeat at the hands of the PPP. Of the 24 seats contested, the PPP won 18, the NDP won two, and the remaining four were won by independents. The success of the NDP, as Despres has noted, may have been in the fact that it was able to affix the communist label indelibly on the PPP and to draw the attention of both the British and the American governments to the possibility of a communist takeover in Guyana.[32]

THE EVICTION OF THE PPP FROM OFFICE

As a result of its victory in the national elections, the PPP was accorded the privilege of naming six ministers to the Executive Council. However, a dispute developed between Forbes Burnham and Cheddi Jagan, not only over the question of who should be appointed to ministerial positions, but also over the question of who should be appointed to the position of leader of the Legislative Assembly. The position carried the trappings, if not the power, of a prime minister. Forbes Burnham made a bid for that position but was not supported by the party executive, and Cheddi Jagan was accorded the title. A compromise list of ministers was then worked out between Cheddi Jagan and Forbes Burnham. Cheddi Jagan became the Minister of Agriculture; Forbes Burnham, Minister of Education; Ashton Chase, Minister of Labor; Sydney King, Minister of Communications and Works; J. P. Latchmansingh, Minister of Health; and Jai Narine Singh, Minister of Local Government.[33]

Conflict soon developed between the PPP ministers and the British governor as the PPP proceeded to implement its program. The PPP ministers lacked experience. The blame for this rested squarely on the shoulders of the British. After all, the system by which the colony was administered had not, until now, permitted genuine representatives of the people to participate in the decision-making process. The PPP ministers took office with an exaggerated view of what they could accomplish. They tended to be brash and their tactics confrontational. They described themselves not as members of the government but as "the People's Opposition."[34] The British governor was apparently not amused.

There were two bills proposed by the PPP that especially alarmed the governor and sugar interests in the colony. The first was the Rice Farmers' Security of Tenure Bill that sought to guarantee rice farmers security of tenure by protecting them against drastic rent increases and by requiring landlords to provide the tenants with certain services, such as drainage facilities, and to make improvements. To give the legislation teeth, the bill empowered the district commissioner to order landlords to make improvements, and in the event of noncompliance, to carry out the improvements and to charge the costs to the landlords. However, what was particularly alarming to the governor and to the sugar companies, which were the largest landowners in the colony, was the fact that the bill would also give the district commissioner the right of "parate execution." This was an eighteenth century Dutch procedure that empowered the district commissioner to dispose of the property of landlords who did not pay the improvement costs levied against them. The governor and the sugar companies feared that the legislation was aimed at landowners whom the PPP disliked. With this legislation in force, the

PPP could conceivably order improvements beyond the value of the land and force the sale of the land by parate execution. It was well known that the PPP wanted to expropriate the unused lands under the control of the sugar companies. The bill passed in the lower house, the House of Assembly, but was rejected by the upper house, the State Council.[35]

The second bill, which provoked a constitutional crisis, was a labor relations bill whose passage would have given the PPP effective control over the labor movement in Guyana. In 1949, Cheddi Jagan became president of the Sawmill and Forest Workers' Union, a position he retained while he was serving in the government in 1953. There were two other major unions that the PPP wanted to control. The first was the British Guiana Labour Union (BGLU), one of the largest African-dominated unions in the colony. In 1952, the PPP acquired control of this union when Forbes Burnham became its president.[36] The other union that the PPP wanted to control was the sugar union. This was the largest union in the colony and had a predominantly Indian membership. The recognized union, the MPCA, had acquired the reputation as a company union. The PPP leaders hoped to replace the MPCA with the party-sponsored union, the GIWU, by appealing to the political loyalties of the Indians in the sugar industry. Although the GIWU claimed a larger membership than the MPCA, the Sugar Producers' Association refused to recognize the GIWU. In the absence of legal machinery to press the issue, the GIWU resorted to strikes as a way of demonstrating its strength. The first recognition strike had occurred in 1948 when five demonstrating sugar workers were fatally shot by the police at Plantation Enmore.

After the Enmore shooting, the GIWU continued its struggle for recognition in the sugar industry. However, organizational work by its leaders became very difficult because they had been served with trespass notices prohibiting them from going on to the sugar plantations where many of the workers lived. J. P. Latchmansingh, president of the GIWU, was affected by this action and so too was Cheddi Jagan, although the latter was an elected member of the legislature and represented a constituency in which sugar workers predominated.

In November 1952, the GIWU called a recognition strike on the estates on the East Coast of Demerara, where support for the union was strongest. The strike brought three sugar factories to a standstill. Although the strike also got support from the sugar estates on the East Bank, West Bank, and West Coast of Demerara, it did not achieve its purpose. The PPP's electoral victory in April 1953 placed the party in a strategic political position, and the GIWU was encouraged to renew its recognition struggle. From May 5 to May 18, 1953, there was a strike at Leonora Estate, but without any significant gains. On August 31, the GIWU called a general strike on the sugar estates, ostensibly over the question of wages and working conditions. The real purpose was to get the SPA to negotiate with the GIWU. The strike lasted for 25 days and had the support of several other unions, which had called sympathy strikes that coincided with the last few days of the GIWU strike.[37] However, the goal of recognition was not achieved.

Because of the frequency of strikes in the sugar industry, the Minister of Labor held discussions with the Sugar Producers' Association with the hope of arriving at some acceptable solution. As a result, the Sugar Producers' Association agreed to recognize the GIWU for field workers but to continue to recognize the MPCA for the factory workers. This proposal was rejected by the GIWU, which wanted unconditional recognition for all the field and factory workers previously represented by the MPCA. The SPA's counterproposal included the acceptance by the GIWU of all collective agreements made with the MPCA and the execution by the GIWU of similar agreements. After perusing those agreements the GIWU rejected that condition. It reserved the right to negotiate and settle fresh agreements with the SPA. The negotiations were inconclusive. However, the PPP government gave the GIWU and the supporting unions the assurance that it would proceed immediately to introduce the legislation of a labor relations bill to provide for the compulsory recognition of trade unions selected by the workers through a secret poll.[38]

The Labor Relations Bill was introduced and read for the first time in the House of Assembly by the Minister of Labor on September 29, 1953. The bill provided for the compulsory recognition of trade unions based on the preference of the workers as ascertained by means of a secret ballot. In an industry where the workers were not unionized, a union needed 51 percent of the vote to become recognized as the bargaining agent of the workers. However, if a recognized union was being challenged by a new union, the new union had to win 65 percent of the vote in order to replace the old one. The bill also provided penalties for an employer that refused to recognize a union that had obtained a government-issued certificate of recognition as a result of a poll.[39] The bill was passed by the House of Assembly on October 8, 1953. On the following day, however, the constitution was suspended, British troops landed in Guyana, and the PPP was thrown out of the government after only 133 days in office. The British government justified these actions as necessary "to prevent communist subversion of the Government and a dangerous crisis both in public order and in economic affairs."[40]

The PPP was accused of attempting to transform the colony into a communist satellite that could be used as a platform for extending communist influence in the Western hemisphere. To support the accusation, the British government provided details of the PPP's dealings with the international communist movement. However, the immediate cause of the crisis was the Labor Relations Bill, which the British saw, not as a neutral piece of legislation to regulate labor relations, but as an attempt by the PPP to take control of the trade union movement of Guyana and to use it for political purposes.[41] Considering that the governor had constitutional powers, such as the veto, to keep the PPP ministers in check, the measures resorted to by the governor and the British government were unquestionably excessive.

THE BURNHAM-JAGAN SPLIT

The constitutional suspension order and the emergency measures taken by the governor greatly affected the relationship between the two factions of the PPP. The constitutional suspension order made reference to a communist clique within the PPP and named, as its ring leaders, Cheddi and Janet Jagan, Sydney King, and Rory Westmaas.[42] King and Westmaas, as well as Martin Carter, Fred Bowman, and Ram Karran, all of whom were regarded as doctrinaire Marxists closely identified with the Jagan faction, were imprisoned without trial. Cheddi and Janet Jagan were each imprisoned for six months for minor infractions of the emergency regulations. The "moderates" within the party, including Forbes Burnham, were restricted in their movements for a short period of time.[43] The difference in the treatment meted out to the two groups added to the suspicion with which the doctrinaire Marxists viewed their colleagues within the party.

Open conflict erupted within the party in February 1955 when Forbes Burnham made a second bid to secure control of the party. Burnham was no doubt encouraged in this move by the report of the royal commission that came to Guyana in January 1954 to investigate the 1953 constitutional crisis. The Robertson Commission, as it was commonly referred to, concluded that there were two groups within the PPP, a communist group led by the Jagans and a socialist group led by Burnham. The commission thought that the socialists were democrats and issued a challenge to them when it stated: "We doubt however if they [the socialists] had the wit to see the essential difference between themselves and their communist colleagues or the ability to avoid being outmaneuvered by them."[44] Burnham was also urged by conservative elements at home to join with noncommunists like J. P. Latchmansingh and to keep the party together by getting rid of the extremists.[45]

The coup attempt by Burnham involved a vote of no-confidence against the existing party executive and the election of a new one with Burnham as the party leader.[46] The coup failed because only a small segment of the party executive joined him. Burnham was, however, able to draw two prominent Indians, J. P. Latchmansingh and Jai Narine Singh, into his camp. The prominent blacks within the party—Sydney

King, Martin Carter, Ashton Chase, Rory Westmaas, and Brindley Benn—remained with Jagan. The split between Burnham and Jagan was open and irrevocable.

Since the Burnham faction retained the party name, there existed two PPPs, one headed by Burnham and one by Jagan. In August 1957, elections were held under a revised constitution. Both factions of the PPP contested. They were opposed by the United Democratic Party (UDP) led by John Carter and representing middle class blacks, and the National Labour Front (NLF), which was led by Lionel Luckhoo and which was simply the political arm of the sugar union, the MPCA. Both of the latter parties were formed from the National Democratic Party that had fought the 1953 elections. The relatively unknown Guiana National Party also fought the elections, as did several independents. Of the 14 elected seats being contested, the Jagan faction of the PPP won nine, the Burnham faction won three, and the UDP and NLF each won one seat.[47] The governor invited Jagan to name five ministers to serve in the Executive Council.

THE EMERGENCE OF RACIAL POLITICS IN GUYANA

Edgar Thompson has noted that "Plantation societies are notoriously areas of race problems."[48] In this regard, Guyana has not been spared. One of the impacts of the plantation on the demography of Guyana up until the end of World War II was the physical and occupational separation of the Indians and the Africans. Although there were many African villages, Africans also tended to dominate the towns. The Indians, on the other hand, lived in the rural areas and were employed in agriculture. However, by the end of World War II, the Indians had consolidated their position in agriculture and were beginning to move into the towns through commerce, the professions, and the civil service. There was a clear potential for economic competition between the Indians and Africans becoming transmuted into racial conflict. The emergence of the PPP as a multiracial organization contributed immensely to the promotion of racial amity between the Africans and the Indians. However, Burnham's departure from the PPP in 1955 created a situation in which racial appeals could be used to some advantage.

Race began to emerge as an issue of Guyanese politics just before the 1957 elections. In the fall of 1956 Martin Carter and Rory Westmaas left the Jagan faction of the PPP. They were later followed by Sydney King. The resignations were a reaction to Jagan's speech to the party's annual congress in which he suggested that the suspension of the constitution in 1953 had been caused by the ultra-leftists within the party who had become bombastic and were challenging everybody at the same time. Jagan also accused this group of abandoning the party line on the West

Indies Federation issue. The resignations of these blacks, who had been strong Jagan supporters, were a serious blow to the Jagan faction of the PPP because they represented a further erosion of the party's claim to being a multiracial nationalist organization. Sydney King contested the 1957 election as an independent and appeared to have abandoned Marxism for a more racial position.[49]

After the 1957 elections Forbes Burnham renamed his faction of the PPP, the People's National Congress (PNC). Burnham's decision to merge with the small black-dominated United Democratic Party seemed to reflect his acceptance of a more racial basis for future electoral contests. Besides, given the fact that he had broken away from the PPP, which was generally regarded as the repository of socialist doctrine in Guyana, Burnham had to rely on an appeal to the black electorate in order to maintain himself in the political arena.[50] In 1958, Burnham was able to attract Sydney King into the PNC. Burnham had assisted King in the 1957 election campaign. King formally entered the PNC as the party's general secretary as well as the editor of the party's newspaper, *The New Nation*.[51] The PNC was beginning to emerge as the party of the Afro-Guyanese. At the same time, despite Jagan's ability to retain prominent blacks such as Ashton Chase and Brindley Benn within the PPP, the PPP began to acquire the reputation as the party of the Indians. The essence of the new type of politics that was emerging was encapsulated in the term, "apan jhaat" ("vote for your own race"), the use of which had acquired wide currency in the Indian communities.

In March 1960, the British Colonial Secretary held a new constitutional conference for Guyana, which both Jagan and Burnham attended. New elections were to be held in 1961. Provisions were made for a bicameral legislature. The Legislative Assembly, or lower house, would consist of 35 members to be elected on the basis of single-member constituencies. The leader of the majority party would be designated premier and would be invited to set up a cabinet government to handle the internal affairs of the colony. Defense and foreign affairs would continue to be handled by the governor. The premier would also nominate eight of the 13 senators in the Senate, or upper house, with three of the remaining senators nominated by the opposition and two by the governor. The conference rejected Burnham's demand for a change in the electoral system to proportional representation.[52]

After the conference, Burnham renewed his efforts to consolidate the anti-PPP elements behind him. He began to focus on the Portuguese middle class and those in the Indian middle class who felt threatened by the socialist course that Jagan was charting. The spokesman for this group was Peter S. D'Aguiar, a very successful Portuguese businessman who ran a very profitable beer and soft drink business. He had contested the 1953 elections as an independent and was again seeking entry into public life. Talks between Burnham and D'Aguiar began in 1959. D'Aguiar proposed to provide financial assistance to the PNC in exchange for majority control over the PNC's Executive Committee. D'Aguiar promised that he and his supporters would join the PNC and make their membership known to the public. In addition, they would provide the financial backing for a massive election campaign against the PPP. In exchange, D'Aguiar demanded nine of the 15 seats on the PNC's Executive Committee. He would concede the party leadership to Burnham. If the party won the election Burnham would be the premier, but Peter D'Aguiar would become the Minister of Trade and Industry. Burnham was greatly offended by the offer. He accused D'Aguiar of wanting "to buy the party as though it were a box of empties being returned to his brewery."[53]

However, given the kind of support D'Aguiar claimed to have, the Executive Committee of the PNC instructed Burnham to offer D'Aguiar six seats on the Executive Committee, provided D'Aguiar could fill four of these with Indians from the Rice Producers' Association, where D'Aguiar apparently claimed he had a following. D'Aguiar accepted this offer, but since the list of names he submitted only included two Indians from the Rice Producers' Association, the PNC rejected D'Aguiar's list of nominees and terminated the negotiations.[54]

In October, 1960, Peter D'Aguiar launched a new political party, the United Force (UF). The initial pledges of support came mostly from Portuguese and Indian businessmen, and from the Indian leaders of the unpopular sugar union, the MPCA. The new president of the MPCA, Richard Ishmael, was also the president of the Trades Union Council and was potentially a useful ally. However, the MPCA's endorsement of the United Force deprived the party of any serious consideration by the majority of the sugar workers.[55]

The elections were scheduled for August 21, 1961. However, as the election date drew closer, racial tension between the Africans and the Indians increased. It was generally understood that independence would be granted by Britain some time during the four years following these elections. Both Jagan and Burnham were committed to the goal of achieving the independence of Guyana. Burnham had stated that he would insist that the British leave even if he lost the elections to Jagan. The position taken by Burnham was challenged within his own party. Some black leaders were afraid of Indian domination after the colony received its independence. One of these, Sydney King, the PNC general secretary and editor of the PNC journal, *The New Nation*, had by now become the most ardent advocate of black nationalism in Guyana. In July 1961, King proposed that Guyana be partitioned into three zones: an African zone, an Indian zone and a zone for those who wanted to live together. The proposal for partition was roundly condemned for being conceived in racism. Burnham dissociated himself from the proposal by expelling King from the party.[56]

The 1961 election campaign brought out some of the uglier features of "apan jhaat politics." Candidates campaigned at great physical risk. In African villages and in areas where Africans predominated, PPP meetings were frequently disrupted and in some cases the speakers were stoned. PNC candidates were similarly treated in areas with large concentrations of Indians. Nevertheless, the August 21 elections went very smoothly. The PPP emerged with 20 of the 35 seats. The PNC won 11 seats and the UF got the remaining four.[57] Cheddi Jagan was designated premier and invited to form the new government.

BURNHAM'S RISE TO POWER

Jagan's reputation as a socialist and the fears this inspired within the Kennedy administration in the United States accounted for his downfall. Soon after he became premier, Jagan proclaimed Castro to be one of the world's greatest liberators and proceeded to widen trade relations with Cuba.[58] In doing this, Jagan chose to ignore the tense relationship that had developed between the United States and Cuba. The failure of the U.S.-supported Bay of Pigs invasion was still fresh in the mind of President Kennedy. The United States was orchestrating an economic embargo against Cuba and was trying to isolate Cuba diplomatically. Jagan's actions seemed to be in open defiance of the United States and heightened fears in Washington that an independent Guyana under Jagan might follow the path of Cuba. Officials in the U.S. government began to worry about whether Jagan was "recoverable for democracy."[59]

In October 1961, Jagan visited Washington and had the opportunity to allay the fears of the Kennedy administration with regard to the course he intended to chart for an independent Guyana, but his performance only raised doubts. At Jagan's request, the Kennedy administration had agreed to discuss economic assistance to Guyana. On October 15, while Jagan was in Washington, Jagan appeared on the television program, "Meet the Press." He was questioned about his communist commitments by panel member Lawrence E. Spivak. Jagan's responses were circuitous. He never admitted to being a communist, but he never denied it either and he was very reluctant to speak critically of the Soviet Union. President Kennedy, who had tuned in for the last part of the interview, instructed that no pledges of aid should be made until he had spoken to Jagan. In his October 25 interview with Kennedy and his advisers, Jagan failed to convince his hosts that he was anything but communist. He spoke of his admiration for the journal *Monthly Review*, edited by Paul Sweezy, Leo Huberman, and Paul Baran, which Kennedy and his advisers viewed as a procommunist publication. President Kennedy was worried about the future of democracy under Jagan. He said, "I have a feeling that in a couple of years he will find ways to suspend his constitutional provisions and will cut his opposition off at the knees."[60] On the other hand, Burnham made a favorable impression in Washington during May 1962 and the assessment was made that "an independent British Guiana under Burnham (if Burnham will commit himself to a multi-racial policy) would cause us fewer problems than an independent British Guiana under Jagan."[61] It was this assessment that motivated the United States to assume a more activist role in Guyanese affairs.

There is evidence that between 1962 and 1964 the U.S. Central Intelligence Agency fomented strikes and riots in Guyana with the purpose of overthrowing the PPP government.[62] In February 1962, the opposition parties in Guyana organized protest demonstrations in Georgetown against the government's budget. It was an austerity budget drafted by the noted Cambridge economist, Nicolas Kaldor. It attempted to reform the tax system by increasing the tax obligations of the wealthy, and to increase national savings. The budget proposed taxes on capital gains, gifts, net wealth and the turnover on sales, as well as on luxury and semiluxury items, alcoholic and nonalcoholic beverages, and tobacco. The budget also proposed a system of compulsory saving. The saving plan required that 5 percent of salaries over G$100 per month, or 10 percent of incomes and profits from companies and self-employed people, be invested in government bonds paying 3.75 percent interest. The interest was to be tax-exempt and the bonds were redeemable in 7 years.[63]

Forbes Burnham joined Peter D'Aguiar in opposing the budget, and they both rallied their supporters in Georgetown for a showdown with the government. Because the Trades Union Council (TUC) had raised objections to the budget, the government agreed to postpone consideration of the budget until after it had discussed it with the TUC on February 15. However, the TUC called a general strike on February 13. In the demonstrations and riots that followed, large sections of Georgetown were burned down, and looting was widespread. Five people, including a police superintendent, lost their lives and numerous others were injured. Fire insurance claims totalled G$11 million. The government was forced to accede to the demands of the strikers.[64]

The British government used this situation to postpone the conference that was to fix the date for the colony's independence. The conference eventually met in October 1962 in Britain but ended two weeks later because agreement could not be reached by the parties attending. Jagan was demanding that a date for independence be set while his opponents, Burnham and D'Aguiar, insisted that new elections under proportional representation be held before independence was granted and they pointed to the fact that Jagan did not have the support of the majority of the people and should not be allowed to lead the country into independence. The British Colonial Secretary, Duncan Sandys, indicated that if the Guyanese leaders could not reach an agreement and if the domestic situation deteriorated, the British government might impose a solution. None of the three Guyanese leaders wanted this. The British government then decided that the talks should go on but that the place should be Guyana and the governor should be the convener.[65]

The talks with the governor began in late November 1962. Since D'Aguiar was out of the colony, the discussions were principally between Burnham and Jagan. Burnham insisted on elections on the basis of proportional representation before independence. Jagan conceded new elections but insisted on the retention of the present electoral system. Encouraged by this concession, Burnham became obstinate in his demand for a change to proportional representation. At this point Jagan invited Burnham into a coalition government. The correspondence between the two men became protracted and it became clear that Burnham would settle for nothing except a complete capitulation by Jagan.[66]

Correspondence between these two leaders on the coalition proposal was still going on when the TUC called a general strike in April 1963. Early in 1963, the PPP renewed its offensive in the labor movement. Under its sponsorship the Guyana Industrial Workers' Union held its first congress in February. At the congress it changed its name to the Guyana Agricultural Workers' Union (GAWU) and pledged to renew its effort to replace the MPCA as the recognized bargaining agent of the sugar workers. Since the PPP realized that the Sugar Producers' Association would not recognize the GAWU in the place of the MPCA, it turned to legislation.

On March 25, the PPP government introduced the Labor Relations Bill which was very similar to the one it had proposed in 1953. The bill proposed to empower the government to conduct a poll in any industry in which there was a jurisdictional dispute between two or more unions.[67] The most immediate effect of such a bill would be a poll in the sugar industry to decide whether GAWU or the MPCA should represent the sugar workers. The PPP was confident that GAWU would win because it was common knowledge that the MPCA did not enjoy the support of the sugar workers and was the recognized union only because the sugar companies preferred it. Besides, the PPP was well entrenched in the sugar belt and the leaders felt that they could persuade the sugar workers to vote for the union enjoying the party's sponsorship.

The Trades Union Council opposed the Labor Relations Bill. Such opposition could have been anticipated since the TUC president, Richard Ishmael, was also the president of the MPCA and stood to lose both positions if the bill was passed and if GAWU replaced his union in the sugar industry. The TUC issued a call for a general strike commencing on May 20. The TUC strike call was virtually ignored in the rural areas. Of the 20,000 sugar workers claimed by the MPCA, only about 2,000 responded. However, the others were locked out by the sugar companies, which opposed the bill.[68]

The central figure behind opposition to the bill turned out to be Forbes Burnham. Burnham, who had supported a similar bill when he was a PPP minister in 1953, chose to oppose the 1963 bill and rallied his Georgetown supporters behind him. Urban unions sympathetic to the PNC joined the general strike. Prominent among these unions were the Civil Service Association, and the postal and transport unions. Peter D'Aguiar played a supporting role during the strike. He used the trucks from his beer and soft drink business to shuttle demonstrators back and forth.[69]

The introduction of the Labor Relations Bill became the occasion for massive U.S. intervention against the PPP government. The success of this intervention was due largely to the fact that the United States enjoyed a significant degree of penetration of Guyana's labor movement. The MPCA was an affiliate of the International Confederation of Free Trade Unions (ICFTU), the anticommunist counterpart of the World Federation of Trade Unions (WFTU). The fact that the GAWU was affiliated to the WFTU guaranteed the MPCA of ICFTU support. Apart from the benefits of formal ICFTU membership, the MPCA had also found a very useful ally in Serafino Romualdi, who headed the Western Hemisphere division of the ICFTU and was a self-proclaimed opponent of Jagan and the PPP. Romualdi was instrumental in lining up the support of the U.S. labor conglomerate, the AFL-CIO, behind the MPCA.[70] In fact, during the 1962 strike, the AFL-CIO and its Latin American affiliate, the Inter-American Regional Organization of Workers (ORIT), provided large amounts of food to the strikers.[71] In 1961, when the U.S. government and the AFL-CIO established the American Institute for Free Labor Development (AIFLD), Romualdi became the director. The AIFLD was able to secure considerable penetration of the Guyanese labor movement. The AIFLD arranged for Latin American unionists to attend a three-month course in the United States. Participants were then kept on the AIFLD payroll for an additional nine-month period. Several Guyanese trade unionists participated in the AIFLD program. By the time of the 1963 general strike, most of the MPCA officials had passed through the AIFLD program.[72]

Guyanese trade union leaders received considerable encouragement and support from the United States prior to, as well as during, the 1963 general strike. Before the strike, Harvard Professor Dunlop and two AFL-CIO lawyers visited Guyana for the purpose of advising local labor leaders on the Labor Relations Bill. On April 19, two additional U.S. labor officials arrived in Guyana and held an all-night meeting with TUC president, Richard Ishmael, at his Belvidere Hotel.[73]

The ICFTU used its International Trade Secretariats (ITS) to support the general strike. The ITS are international federations of unions operating in the same or related industries. The Public Service International (PSI) Secretariat, whose Guyana affiliate was the Civil Service Association (CSA), played a major role in this strike. The PSI served as a cover for the U.S. Central Intelligence Agency. Howard McCabe, who represented the PSI in Guyana, and who worked actively with local labor leaders during the strike, was believed to have been a CIA operative. The CIA used the PSI secretariat to channel funds to the strikers. Funds were transferred from the CIA to the PSI through a paper organization known as the Gotham Foundation.[74]

The CIA spent over 1 million dollars on the strike. Through the PSI, the CIA paid the salaries of the CSA leaders during the strike.[75] Indeed, the strikers were so well financed that they appeared unwilling to see an end to the strike. They made new demands each time the PPP government gave in to their original ones. The British Trades Union Congress sent Robert Willis, general secretary of the British Typographical Union, to mediate the strike. Willis described the intransigence of the striking unions as follows: "If Dr. Jagan had called me and told me that the unions could write their own demands and he would agree to them, the TUC would still find reasons for not accepting them."[76]

The strike lasted 80 days and was accompanied by demonstrations and violence in and around Georgetown. Opposition handbills encouraged their followers to commit acts of violence.[77] Nine people were killed and numerous others wounded. The strike ended on July 8 with a clear capitulation by the PPP government. The Labor Relations Bill was allowed to lapse and the government agreed not to reintroduce it without consulting with the TUC.[78]

American intervention in Guyana also took the form of direct pressure on the British government to change the colony's electoral system to proportional representation. Given the ethnic composition of the colony and the ethnic voting pattern, a change in the electoral system seemed to the United States to be the most obvious way of removing the PPP from office. In the 1961 election, the PPP had won a majority of the seats in the legislature with 42.6 percent of the popular vote while the PNC and the UF gained 41 percent and 16.3 percent respectively.[79] Under a system of proportional representation, the PPP could be expected to increase its percentage share of the popular vote but was unlikely to attain the 50 percent required to give it control of the government. The opposition parties could then be persuaded to form a coalition government.[80] The British government agreed to the Kennedy administration's proposal to introduce proportional representation into Guyana.[81] This decision sealed the fate of the PPP and set the stage for Burnham's elevation to power.

The opportunity to change the electoral system in Guyana presented itself at the constitutional conference convened by the British Colonial Secretary, Duncan Sandys, at Lancaster House in England in October 1963. The conference began on October 22 and became deadlocked shortly afterwards.[82] Forbes Burnham and Peter D'Aguiar, buoyed by their triumph during the 80-day strike and by the realization that their control over Georgetown rendered the Jagan government a virtual captive, and reassured by the not-too-friendly attitude of the Kennedy administration toward the Jagan government, took up very intransigent positions and rejected all of the compromises suggested by Jagan. Burnham and D'Aguiar demanded new elections before the granting of independence, a change in the electoral system to proportional representation, and a retention of the current voting age of 21. Jagan appeared willing to agree to fresh elections before independence but wanted a retention of the current electoral system of single-member constituencies and a reduction of the voting age to 18. Frustrated by the lack of progress at the conference, Jagan made the biggest blunder of his political career. He proposed that British Colonial Secretary Duncan Sandys provide a solution, and he agreed to sign a letter drafted by Sandys that would acknowledge Sandys' authority to do so. Burnham and D'Aguiar readily endorsed the proposal. The Sandys letter acknowledged the inability of the Guyanese leaders to reach an agreement on the constitutional issues to be settled before Guyana received its independence. These issues were identified as the type of electoral system, the voting age, and the question about whether fresh elections should be held before independence. "In the circumstances," the letter continued, "we are agreed to ask the British Government to settle on their authority all outstanding constitutional issues, and we undertake to accept their decisions."[83] On October 31, Sandys handed down his solution: proportional representation would replace the prevailing system of single-member constituencies, the voting age would remain at 21, and new elections would be held in 1964, after which a conference would be convened in London to fix a date for independence. In effect, Sandys conceded everything that Burnham and D'Aguiar had demanded.

The Sandys decision provoked another major crisis in Guyana. The PPP organized a series of protest rallies against what they viewed as a one-sided settlement. They were determined to prevent the imposition of proportional representation. At the rallies, PPP leaders called on their supporters to be prepared to make every sacrifice to stop proportional representation. The PPP leadership had apparently reasoned that since the British government had intervened as a result of the disturbances instigated by the opposition parties in 1962 and 1963, a second intervention could be forced on the British government if the PPP could cause sufficient disruption. Brindley Benn, chairman of the PPP, hinted about where the pressure would be applied when he threatened that the PPP could shut down the sugar industry for 80 weeks.[84]

The PPP carried out its threat in February 1964. From mid-February to August 1964, there was a general strike in the sugar industry. The stated purpose of the strike was to win recognition for the PPP-backed sugar union, the Guyana Agricultural Workers' Union. However, it was clear that the strike was also politically motivated. The sugar strike was the mechanism that the PPP intended to use to stop the Sandys plan. But the PPP leadership was also looking ahead. If the party lost the next election, and there was good reason to believe that it would under the system of proportional representation, control over the recognized sugar union would put the PPP in a powerful position vis-à-vis future governments. A collateral benefit would come from the influence GAWU would exercise within the Trades Union Council.

Both during and after the strike, the country was rocked by waves of terror and racial violence that the PPP could not have anticipated since its supporters suffered the brunt of these. About 176 people lost their lives and about 920 others were injured. Over 1,400 homes were destroyed by fire. About 2,688 families involving approximately 15,000 persons were forced to move their homes and resettle in communities of their own ethnic group.[85]   Neither the PPP nor GAWU achieved any of its primary goals. Although GAWU demonstrated convincingly that it had the support of the overwhelming majority of the sugar workers, it was not granted recognition by the Sugar Producers' Association. The British Colonial Office did not change its position with respect to proportional representation. The new governor, Sir Richard Luyt, a South African and a rabid anticommunist, openly sided with Jagan's opponents. In June, he ordered the detention of 32 persons, most of whom were PPP officials. Since some of the detainees were elected members of the legislature, the PPP lost its majority in that body, and with this handicap prepared for the national elections.

Elections, under the system of proportional representation, were held on December 7, 1964. Voting followed racial lines. The PPP received 45.8 percent of the total vote and was awarded 24 of the 53 seats in the legislature. The PNC received 40.5 percent of the vote and 22 seats, and the UF received 12.4 percent of the vote and 7 seats.[86] Burnham rejected an invitation from Jagan for a PPP-PNC coalition and instead entered into a coalition with the United Force. The PNC-UF coalition government, which was headed by Burnham, took office on December 15. Under this government, the colony received its independence from Great Britain on May 26, 1966.

Ironically, "the struggle" for Guyana's independence was not really a struggle between the Guyanese and the British, since the British government seemed predisposed to granting independence. Delays in setting a date for independence were tactical and were linked to Cold War considerations. Essentially, the British were seeking to leave behind in power in Guyana a party, or as it turned out, a coalition of parties that was acceptable to them and to the United States. In these circumstances, the struggle for independence became transformed into an internal struggle for power, one that resulted in the racial polarization of Guyanese society.

NOTES

1. Sir Cecil Clementi, *A Constitutional History of British Guiana* (London: Macmillan and Co., Ltd., 1937), pp. 400–401. See also Ashton Chase, *A History of Trade Unionism in Guyana, 1900 to 1961* (Ruimveldt, Guyana: New Guyana Company Ltd., 1964), pp. 15–16.

2. Ronald Sires, "British Guiana: The Suspension of the Constitution," *Western Political Quarterly* 7 (December 1954), p. 558.

3. Hugh Tinker, "British Policy Towards a Separate Indian Identity in the Caribbean, 1920–1950," (London: Institute of Commonwealth Studies, no date), p. 6.

4. Chase, *A History of Trade Unionism*, pp. 48–56.

5. The only union to register in the intervening years was the British Guiana Workers League. Its registration was cancelled in 1951. See Chase, *A History of Trade Unionism*, p. 80.

6. *Ibid.*, pp. 85–86.

7. *Ibid.*, pp. 87–90.

8. *Ibid.*, p. 85.

9. Cheddi Jagan, *The West on Trial* (Berlin: Seven Seas Publishers, 1975), pp. 43–54.

10. *Ibid.*, p. 15.

11. *Ibid.*, pp. 54–55.

12. *Ibid.*, pp. 60–61.

13. Chase, *A History of Trade Unionism*, pp. 126, 148.

14. Jagan, *The West on Trial*, pp. 62–64.

15. Simms, *Trouble in Guyana*, pp. 80–81.

16. Jagan, *The West on Trial*, pp. 65–69.

17. Simms, *Trouble in Guyana*, pp. 89–90; Chase, *A History of Trade Unionism*, pp. 141–146.

18. Chase, *A History of Trade Unionism*, pp. 146–147.

19. *Ibid.*, p. 141.

20. *Ibid.*, p. 151.

21. Simms, *Trouble in Guyana*, p. 95.

22. Hugh Springer, "Federation in the Caribbean: An Attempt that Failed," in David Lowenthal and Lambros Comitas, eds., *The Aftermath of Sovereignty* (New York: Anchor Press, 1973), pp. 192–193. See also Douglas G. Anglin, "The Political Development of the West Indies," in David Lowenthal, ed., *The West Indies Federation* (New York: Columbia University Press, 1961).

23. C. A. Nascimento and R. A. Burrowes, eds., *A Destiny to Mould* (London: Longman Caribbean Limited, 1970), pp. xvi-xvii.

24. Ernst Halperin, "Racism and Communism in British Guiana," *Journal of Interamerican Studies* 7 (January 1965), p. 115.

25. Despres, *Cultural Pluralism and Nationalist Politics*, p. 194.

26. Thomas J. Spinner, Jr., *A Political and Social History of Guyana, 1945–1983* (Boulder: Westview Press, 1984), p. 30.

27. Smith, *British Guiana*, p. 169.

28. *Ibid.*

29. Sir James Robertson, chairman, *Report of the British Guiana Constitutional Commission* (London: Her Majesty's Stationery Office, 1954), pp. 25–26; also Jagan, *The West on Trial*. pp. 100–101.

30. Despres, *Cultural Pluralism and Nationalist Politics*, p. 201.

31. Simms, *Trouble in Guyana*, p. 115.

32. Despres, *Cultural Pluralism and Nationalist Politics*, p. 202.

33. Spinner, *A Political and Social History*, pp. 37–38.

34. Simms, *Trouble in Guyana*, p. 113.

35. Despres, *Cultural Pluralism and Nationalist Politics*, pp. 205–206; Simms, *Trouble in Guyana*, pp. 116–117.

36. Jagan, *The West on Trial*, p. 97.

37. Chase, *A History of Trade Unionism*, pp. 207–208.

38. *Ibid.*, pp. 207–208.

39. *Ibid.*, pp. 209–211; Spinner, *A Political and Social History*, pp. 42–43.

40. *The Constitution Suspension ordered on October 8, 1953.* (British Guiana: Bureau of Public Information, 1953), p. 3.

41. *Ibid.*, pp. 23–25.

42. *Ibid.*, p. 3.

43. Jagan, *The West on Trial*, pp. 150–157; Despres, *Cultural Pluralism and Nationalist Politics*, p. 210.

44. Robertson, *Report of the British Guiana Constitutional Commission*, p. 37.

45. Simms, *Trouble in Guyana*, pp. 128–129.

46. Jagan, *The West on Trial*, pp. 162–174. For another view of the proceedings that is more sympathetic to Burnham, see Despres, *Cultural Pluralism and Nationalist Politics*, pp. 210–215.

47. Despres, *Cultural Pluralism and Nationalist Politics*, p. 216; Smith, *British Guiana*, p. 180.

48. Edgar T. Thompson, "The Plantation Cycle and Problems of Typology," in Vera Rubin, ed., *Caribbean Studies: A Symposium* (Seattle: University of Washington Press, 1971), p. 31.

49. Jagan, *The West on Trial*, pp. 175–177; Despres, *Cultural Pluralism and Nationalist Politics*, pp. 218–219; Spinner, *A Political and Social History*, pp. 68–69.

50. This observation was made by Smith, *British Guiana*, pp. 181–182.

51. Despres, *Cultural Pluralism and Nationalist Politics*, p. 252; Spinner, *A Political and Social History*, p. 76.

52. Spinner, *A Political and Social History*, pp. 75–76.

53. Despres, *Cultural Pluralism and Nationalist Politics*, p. 257.

54. *Ibid.*, pp. 257–258.

55. *Ibid.*, p. 258.

56. Spinner, *A Political and Social History*, p. 79.

57. *Ibid.*, p. 81.

58. Ralph R. Premdas, "Guyana: Socialist Reconstruction or Political Opportunism?" *Journal of Interamerican Studies and World Affairs* 20 (May 1978), p. 136.

59. Arthur M. Schlesinger, Jr., *A Thousand Days: John F. Kennedy in the White House* (Boston: Houghton Mifflin Company, 1965), p. 774.

60. *Ibid.*, p. 777.

61. *Ibid.*, pp. 778–779.

62. See Philip Reno, *The Ordeal of British Guiana* (New York:Monthly Review Press, 1964), pp. 34–67; Ronald Radosh, *American Labor and United States Foreign Policy* (New York: Random House, 1969), pp. 393–405; Richard J. Barnet, *Intervention and Revolution* (New York: New American Library, 1972), pp. 280–284; V. Marchetti and J. D. Marks, *The CIA and the Cult of Intelligence* (New York: Dell Publishing Co., 1974), p. 373; Philip Agee, *Inside the Company: CIA Diary* (London: Penguin Books, 1975), pp. 293–406.

63. Jagan, *The West on Trial*, pp. 208–209.

64. *Ibid.*, pp. 220–221.

65. *Ibid.*, pp. 268–274.

66. *Ibid.*, pp. 274–277.

67. Spinner, *A Political and Social History*, pp. 100–101.

68. Reno, *The Ordeal of British Guiana*, p. 54.

69. *Ibid.*, p. 55.

70. *Ibid.*, p. 37.

71. Barnet, *Intervention and Revolution*, pp. 281–282.

72. Reno, pp. 50–52.

73. *Ibid.*, pp. 53–54.

74. Radosh, *American Labor and United States Foreign Policy*, pp. 399–400.

75. *Ibid.*, pp. 400–405; Reno, *The Ordeal of British Guiana*, p. 54.

76. Quoted in Reno, *The Ordeal of British Guiana*, p. 56.

77. For a sampling of the handbills, see Jagan, *The West on Trial*, p. 231.

78. Reno, p. 57.

79. Spinner, *A Political and Social History*, p. 81.

80. Schlesinger, Jr., *A Thousand Days*, p. 779.

81. *Ibid.*, p. 886.

82. Simms, *Trouble in Guyana*, p. 171.

83. *Ibid.*, pp. 171–172.

84. Joseph B. Landis, *Race Relations and Politics in Guyana*, Ph.D. Dissertation (Yale University: Department of Sociology, 1971), pp. 258–262.

85. For details of the violence, see Jagan, *The West on Trial*, pp. 305–312; Spinner, *A Political and Social History*, pp. 105–110.

86. Landis, *Race Relations*, p. 325; Halperin, "Racism and Communism," pp. 131–132.

3

ELECTIONS AND POLITICAL PARTIES

INTRODUCTION

The U.S. Department of State's assessment that the PNC government uses "the form of a parliamentary democracy but not the substance,"[1] finds corroboration in the way the ruling party manages the elections in Guyana. Indeed, an analysis of the elections in postindependence Guyana quickly turns into a catalog of fraud. In each general election, it was known beforehand that the PNC would win. What was usually not known was how many parliamentary seats it would allocate to itself and how many it would assign to its opposition. In each case the PNC emerged with a larger number of seats in parliament, despite a progressive worsening of the social and economic conditions in the country.

The 1964 general election was the last free and fair election in Guyana, at least in the sense that there were no irregularities in the balloting, or in the counting of the ballots. However, the election was conducted under a new electoral system, namely proportional representation. The British Colonial Secretary justified the imposition of proportional representation on the grounds that it would encourage coalition between parties and would make it easier for new political groupings to form on a multiracial basis.[2] In the latter respect, the new system of elections failed. It was clear after the 1961 election that race had become the primary determinant of party identification. Jagan was identified as leader of the Indians and Burnham as leader of the Africans. The 1964 election merely confirmed this. The percentages of the votes polled by the PPP and the PNC approximated the respective percentages of Indians and Africans in the electorate. The introduction of proportional representation led to an intensification of segmentation based on race.

THE 1968 GENERAL ELECTION

In 1963, Harold Wilson, leader of the opposition Labor Party in Britain, referred to the change in the electoral system of Guyana as "a fiddled constitutional arrangement."[3] Wilson's comment had a prophetic ring, in the sense that this turned out to be the first of a series of fiddled electoral arrangements in Guyana. The second occurred in December 1968 when the PNC rigged the general election to give itself a majority of the parliamentary seats.

The PNC-UF coalition that took office in December 1964 was an uneasy one. Burnham was never comfortable with his coalition partner, Peter D'Aguiar, who had called him a communist in the 1961 and 1964 election campaigns. D'Aguiar, who was the finance minister in the coalition government, became outraged by the scale of corruption in the government as the PNC proceeded to reward its supporters. One of the most glaring cases surfaced in 1967 when the director of audits could not produce proper vouchers for approximately G$20 million of government expenditures. D'Aguiar eventually resigned his cabinet position in September 1967.[4]

Toward the end of this legislative term, D'Aguiar and the UF were joining Jagan and the PPP in staging walkouts from the legislative assembly to protest against PNC actions in government. However, by the end of 1968, Burnham had succeeded in inducing a sufficient number of legislative defections from both the PPP and the UF to give him control of the government. He took control of the election machinery and used it to return the PNC to power with a legislative majority.

Several areas of controversy surrounded the conduct of the December 1968 general election. The first concerned the number of registered voters on the domestic electoral roll. The number of electors on the domestic roll in 1968 had increased dramatically from the previous election. Between the 1953 and 1964 elections, the total number of registered voters increased by 40,665. However, between the 1964 and 1968 elections, the number of registered voters had increased by 49,800.[5] The distribution of the increase raised serious doubts about its validity. The average increase over six PPP strongholds in the Corentyne was 10 percent. However, in areas identified as PNC strongholds, the increases were enormous. The increases for the Mackenzie, Mazaruni-Potaro, and Abary districts were 109 percent, 58 percent, and 49 percent, respectively.[6]

A second area of controversy centered around the participation of nonresident voters in the election. The Representation of the People Act of 1968 made provision for people who were born in Guyana but were resident overseas to participate in all future general elections. The first issue in this regard concerned the propriety of permitting people who had left Guyana permanently to participate in the selection of a government under which they would not have to live. The second issue concerned the actual compilation of the overseas register, more specifically, its size and validity. While the domestic register totaled 297,404, the overseas register produced an additional 70,541 eligible voters and had the effect, therefore, of increasing the domestic roll by 23.7 percent.[7] The overseas electoral list showed that there were 45,000 Guyanese living in Britain in 1968. However, British census figures showed that the number of Guyanese living in Britain in 1968 was just over 20,000. The Opinion Research Centre in England conducted a survey of the names listed by the Guyana government as overseas Guyanese qualified to vote. Acknowledging a sampling error of 3 percent, the Research Centre concluded that only about 15 percent of the names on the overseas electoral roll for Great Britain were valid. It also found that 25 percent of the addresses did not exist, and that when the addresses did exist, about 41 percent did not house the individual listed and 1 percent did not house Guyanese. Humphrey Taylor, director of the Opinion Research Centre, concluded that the compilation of the electoral list for Great Britain was "a totally dishonest and corrupt operation."[8] Not surprisingly, the PNC received approximately 95 percent of the total overseas vote.

Controversy also arose over the use of proxy votes. In the 1964 general election, the governor of the colony had permitted a more extended use of proxy voting than had previously been the case. There were no irregularities in the use of the proxy vote then, but this component of the election machinery caught the attention of a Commonwealth team that was observing the conduct of that election. In its final report the team warned that the proxy system of voting was liable to abuse.[9] In the 1968 general election this fear was realized. The total number of proxy votes cast in the 1964 election amounted to 7,000 and accounted for 2.5 percent of the total votes cast. In the 1968 election, when one person could vote for up to five electors, there were 19,297 proxy votes accounting for 7 percent of the total votes cast and equivalent to 2 of the 53 seats in the national assembly.[10] The law required that the list of proxies be published four days before election day. This was not done and, in fact, no such list has ever been published.[11]

A fourth area of controversy revolved around the counting of the ballots within Guyana. Prior to the 1968 election, the counting of the ballots took place at each of the electoral districts. For the 1968 election, however, three locations were designated as centers for the counting of the ballots. This meant that the ballot boxes had to be transported over long distances, and the opposition parties feared that the ballot boxes might be tampered with, especially since representatives from the opposition parties were not allowed to accompany the boxes to the counting centers. Opposition fears were justified. In one box for the Pomeroon district there were four wads of ballot papers bound by rubber bands! In several other boxes there were discrepancies between the number of ballots in the box at the time of counting and the number of cast ballots recorded when the polls closed.[12]

Finally, the PNC government had mounted an elaborate campaign prior to election day to ensure that each voter would have an identification card with his or her photograph and fingerprints. However, many of these identification cards were not distributed until election day, several days after the overseas votes and the proxy votes had been administered.[13] The lack of uniformity of procedures and the discretionary powers apparently conferred on officials handling certain areas of balloting cast additional suspicion on the fairness of the election.

THE 1973 GENERAL ELECTION

The 1973 election was conducted in a manner very similar to the 1968 election except that the scale of fraud was even greater. Prior to the election, the PNC repeatedly announced that it would win two-thirds of the seats in the national assembly. This set the level of electoral manipulation. The party was intent on getting a two-thirds majority because this was what was needed to change certain provisions in the constitution.

Two new parties entered the electoral contest. The less significant was the People's Democratic Movement (PDM) led by Llewellyn John. John had been the Minister of Home Affairs in the PNC government in 1968 and had been responsible for overseeing the conduct of the election held that year. He subsequently broke with Burnham when Burnham began to take the PNC leftward. John, who is an Afro-Guyanese, spent much time in Berbice campaigning among the Indians. Obviously embarrassed by his former association with the PNC, he ran an artless campaign, in which he quietly tried to convince Indians that he had the backing of the American CIA and was therefore the only one who could unseat the PNC.[14]

The other party was the Liberator Party (LP), led by Ganraj Kumar, an Indian physician, and Makepeace Richmond, a black dentist. The LP was a Georgetown-based party that attracted the well-to-do. Businessmen and urban-based professionals, who were not associated with either the PPP or the PNC, chose to identify with the LP. The LP wanted a restoration of a true parliamentary democracy in Guyana. The party supported an economy based on free enterprise and saw an important role for foreign investment in the development of the country. The party leadership was able to persuade Fielden Singh, leader of the United Force, to bring the UF within the structure of the Liberator Party. Despite its ideological orientation, the LP worked very closely with the PPP prior to the election in an effort to ensure that the election would be free and fair.

None of the opposition parties stood a chance in this election because issues did not determine the end result. The electoral machinery was simply rigged to produce a PNC victory. There were, however, some modifications of the measures that had produced the 1968 victory. Embarrassed by the revelations of fraud in the compilation of the overseas register for the 1968 election, the PNC government compiled a new overseas voting register. The size of the eligible electors overseas was reduced by about 50 percent. However, there was a stunning increase in the domestic electoral roll from 297,404 in 1968 to 384,434 in 1973, an increase of 25 percent.[15] The PNC employed the proxy and postal voting mechanisms to its advantage. PNC activists went on a door-to-door campaign in traditional opposition strongholds and, through a combination of promises and threats, tried to get eligible voters who suffered no impediment that would have necessitated their use of a proxy vote to sign a proxy form turning over their vote to the PNC.[16] Signatures on many proxy forms were forged and, as a result, legitimate voters were prevented from casting a ballot on election day because they were told that the records showed that they had already voted by proxy. Postal voting was similarly abused. The results from the overseas votes, the proxy votes, and the postal votes showed that the PNC obtained over 90 percent in each category.[17]

The opposition parties had insisted that the ballots be counted in each electoral district. However, the PNC was adamant; the ballot boxes would be taken to the three centers designated for counting. As in the 1968 election, representatives from the opposition parties were not allowed to accompany the ballot boxes to the counting centers. On election day, July 16, two PPP supporters were fatally shot by members of the Guyana Defense Force as they were protesting the removal of the ballot boxes from a polling station at No. 64 Village on the Corentyne coast. They were apparently implementing Jagan's preelection exhortation to his supporters that they form human barriers around the polling stations to force the government to count the ballots at these stations. The strategy failed. The Guyana Defense Force and the police did not hesitate to use force to remove the ballot boxes from the electoral districts.

One distinctive feature of the 1973 election was the role played by the Guyana Defense Force. Large numbers of the ballot boxes were inexplicably quarantined for over 24 hours at Camp Ayanganna, the headquarters of the Guyana Defense Force, before they were taken to be counted. The PNC leadership resorted to this measure out of fear that the election was not progressing as it had hoped. The party had expected massive wins in its traditional strongholds in Georgetown and had permitted a fair count in several of these constituencies.[18] However, preliminary results showed very low voter turnouts, and the party feared that it would not get the massive victory it had hoped for unless it resorted to extraordinary measures. Accordingly, it used the predominantly black Guyana Defense Force to aid it in committing the foul deed.

In what the *Catholic Standard* called "Fairytale Elections," the PNC obtained 70.1 percent of the votes and awarded itself 37 parliamentary seats. This was slightly over the two-thirds majority it had said it would win. The PPP obtained 26.5 percent of the votes and was awarded 14 seats. The remaining 2 seats went to the Liberator Party which received 2.7 percent of the votes. The PDM, which received 0.6 percent of the votes, was not awarded any seat.[19] Ric Mentus, editor of *The Sunday Graphic*, in a commentary on the election wrote:

The people cannot stretch credulity far enough to embrace both the details of irregularities that they have experienced and the persistent suggestion and in-doctrination that has been coming from all official and semi-official circles. The mind boggles at the enormity of the task, and the Guyanese, after the election, is sadder and a bit more fearful of the future.

If he dares to think about the matter at all, he cannot help coming to the conclusion that whatever was responsible for the stunning victory we have witnessed, it was not fairplay.[20]

Because of pressure from the PNC government, Mentus was removed from his position with the newspaper.

After the results of the election became public, the leaders of the PPP and the Liberator Party agreed to a boycott of Parliament. However, Fielden Singh, former leader of the UF and now deputy leader of the Liberator Party, withdrew the UF out of its alliance with the Liberator Party, and together with former UF member Elenor Da Silva, assumed the parliamentary seats assigned to the Liberator Party. Singh was then appointed Leader of the Opposition in Parliament, a title normally re-served for the leader of the nonruling party with the largest number of seats. The Liberator Party challenged the legality of Fielden Singh's action, but the chief justice, a PNC government appointee, ruled that Fielden Singh had acted legally. The assumption of these two seats in Parliament provided a small measure of legitimacy to the regime, and the PPP was left to continue the boycott by itself. None of the parties that contested the election chose to challenge the electoral proceedings in court because they were convinced that they would not get a fair hearing.

GUYANA'S SOCIALIST PARTIES

The Ruling PNC

Until his death in August 1985, Forbes Burnham dominated the PNC, which he founded in 1957. To party members and prudent government officials, Burnham was known as "the Comrade Leader." Referring to the personality cult that had developed around Burnham, Walter Rodney said, "They have seriously promoted him as the ultimate in wisdom, all-knowing, all-powerful, next to God."[21]

The PNC has the distinction of having undergone the most ideological somersaults of any political party in Guyana. In each case it was Burnham who dictated the change. After his break with Jagan in 1955 Burnham sublimated the socialist beliefs he had hitherto professed. In fact, between 1961 and 1964, he collaborated actively with the capitalist-oriented United Force and accepted help from the CIA to create difficulties for the PPP government in power. Indeed, Burnham came to power in Guyana largely as a result of U.S. opposition to Jagan and the PPP. During the period 1964–1968, Burnham chose the slogan "consultative democracy" to describe the orientation of the coalition government that he led. By this means he hoped to reassure his foreign backers that they had made the right choice and that parliamentary democracy and free enterprise were safe under his political stewardship. It was also prudent because Burnham did not want any further impediment placed in the path to independence.

After the 1968 election Burnham reassumed a socialist posture and the PNC began to advocate cooperative socialism. As Burnham himself put it:

> The People's National Congress is a socialist party. Socialist, not in terms of any European or North American definition which others may seek to thrust upon us, but in terms of our own social needs and wants in creating a just society for the people of Guyana....
>
> A just society cannot be achieved unless the majority of the people, the masses, the little men, have a full share in the ownership and control of the economy, a share which corresponds realistically with their political power.[22]

The party decided that the cooperative was the best vehicle for achieving "a just society" in Guyana. To use the party slogan, the cooperative is the institution through which the "SMALL MAN CAN BECOME A REAL MAN."[23]

The cooperative has been touted as the institution that would achieve the maximum participation of the masses and reduce the likelihood of alienation. The PNC has argued that "cooperatism, conceived in both its organizational and psychological forms, is rooted in the psyche of our people and can best fulfill our developmental goals."[24] The party justifies this belief historically by reference to the early attempts by the exslaves of Guyana to set up cooperative villages after they had left the plantations, and also by reference to the success of extended families within Indian farming communities.[25] To underscore the important role that cooperatives will play in Guyana, the PNC government proclaimed the official title of the country to be the Co-operative Republic of Guyana. In his Declaration of Sophia address, Burnham said:

On the 23rd of February, 1970, Guyana became the first Co-operative Republic in the world and the first Republic in the Commonwealth Caribbean.

Ours is not the first or only government in the developing world to place emphasis on the use and development of the co-operative as an instrument of development or in the thrust towards socialism.

We, however, named *Guyana* a *Co-operative Republic* to highlight the fact that the Co-operative will be the principal institution for giving the masses the control of our economy, to emphasize the fact that we aim at making the Co-operative sector the dominant sector and that the Co-operative is and will be the mechanism for making the *little man a real man.*[26]

One of the principal figures behind the adoption by the PNC of co-operative socialism as its official ideology was Eusi Kwayana. Kwayana was the former Sydney King who decided to cast off his "European slave name" and to adopt the name Eusi Kwayana, which is the Swahili for "Black man of Guyana." Kwayana headed the Association for Social and Cultural Relations with Independent Africa (ASCRIA). ASCRIA was formed in 1964 to revive African culture in Guyana and to stimulate pride among Afro-Guyanese in their African heritage. Another of AS-CRIA's major objectives was to persuade Afro-Guyanese to return to the land. ASCRIA saw the cooperative as the vehicle for accomplishing this.[27] It should be noted that cooperative socialism bore a strong resemblance to ujamaa socialism that Julius Nyerere was practicing in Tanzania in the 1960s. Ujamaa was a "villagization" program based on kinship communalism.[28] Given ASCRIA's purpose and its links with independent Africa, Kwayana may have been influenced by this African form of socialism.

Kwayana was readmitted into the PNC following the party's victory in the 1968 election. ASCRIA became the party's cultural arm, and the PNC leadership was attracted to cooperative socialism because it was an innocuous form of socialism: one that was claiming indigenous roots, that did not promise to embrace the Soviet bloc, and therefore, one that would not provoke a strong reaction from the United States.

Cooperative socialism has come under attack from several quarters. Non-Africans avoid involvement in cooperatives. They view the cooperatives as mechanisms used by the PNC to channel funds to the faithful. Jagan criticizes cooperative socialism as a revisionism of Marxism-Leninism.[29] Sackey argues that cooperative socialism is inconsistent with Marxism-Leninism because the latter aims to give ownership and control over the means of production to the working class while, in Guyana, cooperative socialism had led to the rapid expansion of state capitalism. Sackey also argues that the cooperative approach is being recommended on the basis of a highly selective approach to historical analysis that leads to a distortion of reality. He points out that the postemancipation cooperative movement was produced by a hostile environment and was, therefore, a means of survival.[30] The wisdom of placing such great emphasis on the cooperative has also been questioned by Paul Singh, who has pointed out that most of the postemancipation cooperatives failed.[31]

These criticisms notwithstanding, the PNC stayed the course and used socialism to justify the nationalizations that it carried out. The first of these occurred in July 1971, when the government took over the Demerara Bauxite Company (DEMBA), a subsidiary of the Aluminum Company of Canada. DEMBA had refused to accommodate the government's request to acquire 51 percent of the company's equity. In 1974, the Burnham government nationalized Reynolds Bauxite Company, a subsidiary of Reynolds Metals Company of the United States. Reynolds presented a greater challenge than DEMBA because it was symbolic of Burnham's benefactor, the United States government, to which Burnham had given the assurance that private investment would be promoted and protected.[32] The nationalization of Reynolds implied a break in the relatively close ties Burnham had maintained with Washington. Thereafter, Guyana's ties with Cuba and Eastern bloc countries intensified.

Nationalization of foreign enterprises extended beyond the bauxite industry. In 1975, the government nationalized Jessel Securities Ltd., a British-owned sugar company. It also took over the Thompson-owned daily newspaper, *The Graphic*, and the remaining private radio station, Radio Demerara.[33] Privately run church schools were also brought under state control. By the end of the year, the only major foreign-owned company not under government ownership was Booker Brothers McConnell and Co. Ltd., the British sugar conglomerate. This company alone had generated 25 percent of the country's GNP in 1975. The government nationalized "Bookers" in May 1976 on the tenth anniversary of Guyana's independence. It followed up this action by nationalizing the drug distribution system.[34] By its own reckoning, the PNC government controlled 80 percent of the country's economy.[35]

Control over the economy has increased the ability of the PNC to reward the faithful. For non-Africans seeking certain types of government jobs, possession of a PNC party card has become a prerequisite. In fact, a party card can be very useful in assisting the holder to get a vacancy largely because of the intimidation effect it has over the prospective employer. Control over the economy has also extended the reach of the party over supporters of opposition groups. Punitive transfers and even dismissals are not uncommon.

As the scale of nationalization increased, so did the party's socialist rhetoric. In his address to the first biennial congress of the PNC in August 1975, Forbes Burnham declared the PNC to be "the Vanguard

Party" of Guyana, a title that the PPP traditionally claimed.[36] In his 1976 "Report to the Nation," Burnham announced that "the People's National Congress is seeking to lay the foundations for the establishment of a socialist society based on Marxism-Leninism."[37] Until that time, the PNC had carefully avoided any claims to being a Marxist-Leninist party. Burnham's pronouncement reflected an irreconcilability with the United States and a need to acquire greater acceptability with the Eastern bloc nations.

In order to impart further ideological training to the party personnel, the PNC established the Cuffy Ideological Institute. The Institute was headed by Ranji Chandisingh, who, until his defection to the PNC in 1976, was the PPP's foremost socialist theoretician. Burnham emphasized the necessity for party personnel to participate in the ideological programs of the Cuffy Ideological Institute in order to become grounded in socialist ideology at the practical and theoretical levels.[38] However, despite Burnham's exhortation that the ideological training was also vital because "the members of a Vanguard Party must go beyond an emotional attachment, beyond the attraction of a charismatic leader,"[39] the cult of personality was already firmly established. All strands of power led to Burnham.

Party tranquility was temporarily shattered on August 6, 1985, when Forbes Burnham died of a heart attack. The open struggle for the top position that many observers expected to occur did not materialize. Desmond Hoyte, the prime minister under President Burnham,[40] was elevated by the party executive to become leader of the PNC and president of the country. Hoyte, who was 57 years old on assuming the presidency, is a lawyer by profession. He became a member of Parliament for the first time in 1968. He served in several key ministerial positions such as Home Affairs and Economic Development before being appointed to the post of prime minister in August 1984.[41] Hoyte was a loyal Burnhamite. However, after he became president, he moved considerably to the right.

The principal challenge for the leadership position was expected to come from Hamilton Green. Green headed the party's right wing and developed a reputation as a black nationalist. He has been with the party since 1957. He served for 12 years as the general secretary of the PNC and developed a very strong following among the party rank and file. He was, no doubt, helped by the fact that his late wife, Shirley Field-Ridley, served as Minister of Education and, at the time of her death, was the Minister of Information. She was also a leading figure in the Women's Revolutionary Socialist Movement (WRSM), the women's auxiliary of the PNC. Green himself served in several ministerial positions, including the Ministry of Cooperatives and National Mobilization. At the time of Burnham's death, Green was one of the four vice-presidents and the deputy prime minister. He has established strong links with the military and para-military forces in Guyana, and is reputed to control a private thug force. Although Green only has a secondary school education, he is known to be one of the most ambitious men within the party hierarchy. Surprisingly, he did not put up any visible resistance to Hoyte's elevation to the top position. Instead, Green accepted the position of prime minister, which makes him next in the line of succession.

It was widely believed that Burnham had been grooming his son-in-law, Richard Van West Charles, a Cuban-trained medical doctor and Minister of Health and Public Welfare, for the top leadership position.[42] However, Van West Charles was a relative newcomer to the party and his rise within the party was not viewed very kindly by some senior party officials, particularly by Hamilton Green. Burnham was in the process of containing Green when he died. In August 1984, Prime Minister Ptolemy Reid resigned because of poor health, but instead of appointing Green to that position as had been expected, Burnham appointed Desmond Hoyte. Hoyte may have simply been holding down this position until Van West Charles' preparation was complete. Unfortunately for the latter, Burnham died a year later and Hoyte was appointed party leader.

Uncertain about the strength of support that he had within the party, as well as outside of it, Hoyte tried to capitalize on feelings of sympathy for the fallen "Comrade Leader." The Hoyte government undertook to embalm Burnham's body for permanent viewing and enlisted Soviet help for the task. Hoyte also appointed Burnham's wife, Viola, to the cabinet as the Vice-President for Social Development. Further, in an obvious effort to retain the support of the army, Hoyte promoted the Chief of Staff, Brigadier General Norman McLean to the rank of major general, and the Force Commander, Colonel David Granger, to the rank of brigadier general.[43]

The PPP in Opposition

The People's Progressive Party is a pro-Soviet communist party. Ever since the departure of Forbes Burnham in 1955 the Jagans—Cheddi and his wife, Janet—have dominated the party. Despite the socialist ideology of the party leadership and the socialist image that the party projects domestically and internationally, the party draws its support predominantly from the Indians of Guyana. The support of this capitalist-oriented ethnic community for the socialist PPP is based on ethnic identification with the party leadership.

After the 1964 election, the PPP spent over a year trying to recuperate from its defeat. The party's slogan was "Cheated Not Defeated." A large contingent of its leadership was being detained under the National Security Act, and a considerable amount of its effort went into the campaign to secure their release.

A struggle developed within the party over the strategy that the party should pursue. Certain elements within the party advocated revolutionary action. Cheddi Jagan, the party leader, seemed to have no clear position. In 1963, he had said that he would emulate Fidel Castro if necessary. By 1965, he was not prepared to do that. Instead, he accepted the advice of foreign socialists that he should work within the system and purge "the extremists" from the party. Brindley Benn, the party chairman, was ejected from the party. Moses Bhagwan, chairman of the Progressive Youth Organization (PYO), left the party, as did 11 other members of the PYO executive.[44] There were other party notables, such as C. V. Nunes and H. J. M. Hubbard, former ministers in the PPP government, who retired from politics for different reasons. The party drifted along until the 1968 election.

The PPP had entertained high hopes of winning the 1968 general election. However, after observing the irregularities in the conduct of that election, the party leadership realized that their stay in the opposition might be permanent. Since the country was now independent, and since Cheddi Jagan felt that he did not have to play up to either the British or the United States government, he publicly declared the party to be a Marxist-Leninist party. In June 1969, Jagan formally enrolled the PPP in the communist movement when he attended the Moscow Conference of World Communist Parties.[45] The PPP outlined an "all-embracing anti-imperialist pro-socialist" program which, among other things, called for the nationalization of the economy, workers' participation and control, imbuing the people with the Marxist-Leninist ideology, and closer relations with the socialist world.[46] After the PNC announced that cooperative socialism would be its ideology, the PPP assumed the role of the socialist gadfly, trying to quicken the pace of the socialist transformation of the country. Nevertheless, since its defeat in 1964, the party has come up with no innovative strategy for achieving control of the government. In large measure this is due to the fact that, with its control over the election machinery and the military and paramilitary forces, the PNC has become a formidable foe. However, part of the explanation lies in the quality of leadership. Apart from the Jagans, there are no other individuals of any distinction in the party's central committee. Many in the party executive have very little formal education. New inductees with promise are given some ideological training at Accabre College, the party's ideological center on Regent Street. Some are then sent to Eastern bloc countries, particularly the Soviet Union, for further training in political economy and trade unionism. With very little competition around them, the Jagans exercise firm control over the party. Loyalty is rewarded and mediocrity pervades the party organization. Even though it is out of office, the party still controls some limited patronage. The salary of a parliamentarian is substantial, and loyal supporters can be given the seats that the party picks up in the general elections. Also, the PPP controls the 18,000 member sugar union. Managing the union funds also adds to the patronage potential of the party leadership. There are numerous salaried positions within the union and these are usually assigned to party loyals.

After the 1973 election, the PPP mounted a campaign in which it called for civil disobedience and noncooperation with the government. The success of the campaign rested especially on the willingness of the farming areas that sandwiched Georgetown and that were traditional PPP strongholds to withhold their produce from the Georgetown area. It was never clear whether the PPP leadership realistically believed that this abridged form of Maoist guerrilla warfare would bring down the government, though some party officials talked about this possibility. The civil disobedience campaign seemed to be more of an effort to undermine the legitimacy of the government by drawing attention to the electoral malpractices of the PNC. In any event, the campaign simply fizzled out.

By 1975, Burnham's reputation as a socialist rivaled Jagan's. Jagan could no longer continue his unqualified criticism of the Burnham government when the latter was, in fact, implementing policies that had long been advocated by the PPP, such as the nationalization of the bauxite industry and the establishment of diplomatic relations with socialist countries. However, Burnham needed Jagan's help to continue the drive for the socialist transformation of the country. Jagan controlled the sugar and the rice industries, the other pillars of the economy. Also, Burnham feared a backlash from the United States and wanted Jagan's help to withstand external pressures.[47] Fidel Castro was instrumental in bringing the two leaders together and several agreements were worked out. Both men were in Cuba in 1975, and the Cubans were well represented at the annual congresses of the PPP and the PNC later that year.[48]

At the 25th anniversary conference of the PPP held during the first week of August 1975, Jagan formally abandoned the policy of civil disobedience and noncooperation and declared a policy of "critical support" for the PNC government. He stated:

If we are to arrive at our goal of socialism, imperialism must first be destroyed. And whoever helps must be praised. We must continue to apply pressure on the PNC government and also take our own initiatives in this direction. The situation now therefore demands a more flexible approach on the part of the PPP. The party had previously declared that it does not have a monopoly on socialism, that it is prepared regardless of ideological and tactical differences to work with others if they are interested in building socialism in Guyana, and this includes the PNC.[49]

Jagan also justified the "critical support" line on the ground of self-preservation. He noted that there was a fascist trend in South America and that in each case the communist party was the principal target of "counter-revolutionary blows." Expressing the fear that the progressive moves of the PNC regime could provoke reactionary forces, Jagan said, "It is this possible danger that the PPP sees in the Guyana situation. Our concern is not to save the PNC but to safeguard the interests of the Guyanese nation and people and the lives of the PPP leaders, activists, members and supporters."[50]

Burnham responded by making a major concession in the sugar industry. He allowed a poll to be conducted in the sugar industry to determine which union should be the bargaining agent for the workers. The PPP had long struggled to get such a poll and while in office had attempted to enforce one through its Labor Relations Bills of 1953 and 1963. The poll was conducted on December 31, 1975, and the PPP-backed union, GAWU, won 97.9 percent of the votes cast.[51] Jagan responded by pledging the support of the PPP to the government against any form of external intervention.[52] The PPP also proceeded to take up their 13 seats in Parliament, thereby legitimizing the PNC government.

There were speculations of a possible coalition government, but these did not materialize. Instead, the high point of this entente cordiale was the nationalization of "Bookers" in May 1976. The PNC and the PPP were united on the question of nationalizing the sugar industry. For the PNC government, which was professing socialism, this was the next logical step after the nationalization of the bauxite industry. For Jagan and the PPP, this was an occasion for celebration, since the party had always advocated the nationalization of the sugar industry. However, this seemed to be the extent of PNC-PPP agreement at this time.

The PPP paid a heavy price domestically for its policy of critical support. The Guyana Council of Indian Organizations (GCIO), an amalgam of Indian religious leaders and Indian professionals, which constituted the right wing of the PPP, broke away from the party. The GCIO condemned the PPP for selling out the interests of the Guyana Indians. In Indian communities, the PPP was on the defensive.

The PPP's declaration of critical support for the PNC also became the occasion for the defection of several PPP activists who had been courted for some time by the PNC. The justification that they gave for their departure was that the PNC had become a genuine socialist party and that the PPP's position should have been one of uncritical support for the PNC program and unconditional support for compulsory national service. The defectors accused the PPP leadership of behaving like Trot-skyites.[53]

The defections took Cheddi Jagan and the other top PPP leaders by surprise. Jagan was particularly stung by the defection of Ranji Chandisingh and Vincent Teekah. Chandisingh, a Harvard University graduate, was a long-standing member of the party. He had served in ministerial positions when the PPP was in office. At the time of his defection, he was the assistant general secretary of the party and the party's leading Marxist theoretician. He was immediately admitted into the PNC's Central Executive Committee and was also made the Director of Studies at the Cuffy Ideological Institute. After the promulgation of Guyana's new constitution in 1980, Chandisingh became the Minister of Education, a position he held until 1984 when he was made a vice-president in the PNC cabinet. Chandisingh also became the PNC's general secretary. He retained both positions after Burnham's death.

Chandisingh has been very useful to the PNC. As one who has served in the inner sanctums of the PPP, he fully understands PPP. He can anticipate PPP moves and advise the PNC leadership on counter-moves. At the level of public ideological rhetoric, he has served the PNC in providing the Marxist ripostes to the attacks of the PPP. Chandisingh has lent credibility to the PNC's claim to being a socialist party, yet he has been flexible enough to move with the rightist swings for which this party has a reputation. Since Chandisingh has no grass-root support within the PNC, he poses no threat to the party's predominant black leadership. On the other hand, the fact that Chandisingh and a few other Indians are members of the cabinet and of the party's executive is used by the party leadership to support the claim that the PNC is a genuine multiracial party.

Vincent Teekah, the other PPP defector, had been the chairman of the Progressive Youth Organization, the PPP's youth arm. He was made Minister of Education in the PNC government in 1977. However, on October 24, 1979, Teekah was murdered while in the company of Dr. Oswaldene Walker, Burnham's private dentist. Walker, a Jamaican-born resident of the United States with a practice in Takoma Park, Maryland, was allowed to leave Guyana three days later, and the murder was never solved.[54]

The various defections and the attacks against the PPP on the critical support issue greatly demoralized both the party leaders and the rank and file. The public meetings held around the country by the party during 1975 and 1976 were poorly attended, even in traditional PPP strongholds. By 1977, however, the PPP leaders had regained enough confidence to move from the position of critical support to advocating a national front government of all progressive and anti-imperialist forces in Guyana. Bared of the ideological garb, this was a proposal for power sharing between the PNC and the PPP. The PPP proposed that the president be elected by the people or by the members of the National Assembly, and that the prime minister be drawn from the party or parties with the majority of the seats in the National Assembly. The prime minister would preside over a cabinet consisting of ministers drawn from each party in proportion to its strength in the National Assembly. To ensure balance, the party that wins the National Assembly elections would not oppose the candidature for the presidency from the other major party. The president would have the right of veto over legislation, but there would be provisions for an override by the Assembly.[55] Although various groups, including the churches and the Trades Union Council, advocated some form of power sharing, the PNC rebuffed the idea of a national front government.

The Working People's Alliance

The Working People's Alliance was established in November 1974 as a loose confederation of four political groups: ASCRIA, the Indian Political Revolutionary Associates (IPRA), the Working People's Vanguard Party (WPVP), and Ratoon. ASCRIA, led by Eusi Kwayana, had broken with the PNC in 1971. When it separated itself from the PNC in 1971, ASCRIA admitted that it had unwittingly led Afro-Guyanese into believing that their economic salvation rested with the PNC government, which ASCRIA had hoped would set an example of clean government. Instead, it found that the PNC leaders had become callous, corrupt, and drunk with power. In fact, one of the first acts of Kwayana after he broke with the PNC was to deposit with the ombudsman sworn complaints alleging corruption by two PNC ministers.[56] The PNC countered by reminding people of Kwayana's racial positions in the 1960s. Nevertheless, Kwayana seemed convinced by 1973 that, given the ethnic composition of Guyana and the clear indication that ethnicity determined party identification, no single party could govern the country successfully. Kwayana favored a consociational form of democracy. He embarked on an effort to rehabilitate his political career, which in the previous decade had been built on black militancy. Kwayana decided to link up with an Indian group, the Indian Political Revolutionary Associates, established in 1972 by Moses Bhagwan, a former PPP official. Although IPRA had little following in 1974, it had the potential to attract Indians since Bhagwan was formerly the head of the Progressive Youth Organization, the youth arm of the PPP and was one of the most dynamic personalities ever to head that group. The understanding between IPRA and ASCRIA was that they would each work separately among the Indians and the Africans with the aim of forging a revolutionary alliance between these two ethnic groups.[57]

The WPA was also joined by Brindley Benn, exchairman of the PPP and founder-leader of the Working People's Vanguard Party, a group with few, if any, followers. The Ratoon group that joined the WPA consisted of a handful of University of Guyana lecturers, the most well known of whom were Joshua Ramsammy and Clive Thomas. Both of these men were outspoken critics of the Burnham regime. In 1971, Joshua Ramsammy was shot in what appeared to be an attempt to assassinate him. During the same year, Clive Thomas escaped a kidnapping attempt. The Burnham regime was blamed for the actions against both of these professors.

The prestige of the WPA was considerably elevated when it was joined by the black Marxist historian, Walter Rodney. Rodney became informally identified as the leader of the organization until his assassination in July 1980. Rodney had received his Ph.D. in history from the University of London in 1966, after which he taught at the University of the West Indies at Mona, Jamaica. He first came to the attention of Guyanese in 1968 when he was expelled from Jamaica because of his strong identification with the Black Power movement. He wrote a stirring Black Power primer called *The Groundings With My Brothers*. However, the book that won him acclaim was called *How Europe Underdeveloped Africa*. After his expulsion from Jamaica, Rodney taught at the University of Dar-es-Salaam in Tanzania, where he became a protégé of President Julius Nyerere. In 1974, the Department of History at the University of Guyana offered him the position of department head which he accepted. However, the Burnham government, acting through the Board of Governors of the University, vetoed the appointment. ASCRIA took the lead in organizing protests against the revocation of Rodney's appointment. Public support for Rodney was enormous, but the government was adamant. Rodney returned to live in Guyana in 1975 and joined the WPA.[58]

The WPA started out as an urban-based organization with little mass support. However, largely through the work of Rodney, Kwayana, and Clive Thomas, the WPA was soon able to develop a large following in Guyana's bauxite mining towns of Mackenzie, Kwakwani, and Everton, former strongholds of the PNC. In order to maintain a good working relationship with the PPP, the WPA initially avoided setting up bases in PPP areas.[59]

In 1976, the bauxite workers went on strike. The miners were dissatisfied with the labor agreement signed by the bauxite union, the Guyana Mine Workers' Union. There was also some residual resentment among the workers over the manner in which the election for the executive of the GMWU was rigged to return the pro-PNC leadership. The sugar union, GAWU, called a one-day strike in support of the bauxite workers. The WPA actively supported the strike with Walter Rodney coordinating the entire support effort. What alienated bauxite workers from the PNC was the fact that, during the strike, 42 strikers were arrested and later teargassed in their prison cells. Thereafter, blacks in the mining areas began to dissociate themselves from the PNC, and support for the WPA rose correspondingly.[60]

The WPA is a socialist organization with a socialist program. In describing his political beliefs, Walter Rodney had said, "I aspire to be a Marxist-Leninist."[61] Because of its socialist orientation and because its initial inroads seemed to be in traditional PNC areas, the PPP took the WPA under its wing. Then the WPA began to make inroads into traditional PPP areas. In 1976, Kwayana was recruited by veteran trade unionist Ashton Chase to be the political adviser of the National Association of Agricultural, Clerical, and Industrial Employees (NAACIE). NAACIE is the smaller sugar union that represents the clerical workers in that industry. The Kwayana appointment gave the WPA a footing in the sugar industry.

The WPA was able to put down additional roots in the sugar belt in January 1977, when it endorsed a teachers' strike on the Corentyne coast. The strike was in protest against the arbitrary dismissal of a high school teacher and the transferring of two others. The strike was not sanctioned by the pro-PNC teachers' union, the Guyana Teachers' Association (GTA). However, to the consternation of both the GTA and the government, the strike began to spread and eventually affected the schools in Georgetown. Since the government had given no reasons for its actions, many felt that arbitrary dismissals and transfers were becoming new instruments of intimidation. The WPA supported the teachers at a very early stage. Rodney and other WPA members joined the teachers in picketing activities in the Corentyne and outside of the Ministry of Education in Georgetown.[62] As a result, there was a tremendous amount of goodwill toward Rodney and the WPA in the Corentyne, a traditional PPP stronghold. The WPA subsequently held meetings of its own in this area and the response was tremendous. This tended to be the pattern in other areas as well. Former PPP supporters, who had become tired with the lack of imaginative leadership within the PPP, began to look to the WPA. However, the WPA did not declare itself to be a political party until 1979.

THE REFERENDUM TO END ALL REFERENDUMS

The all-out drive by the PNC to acquire a two-thirds parliamentary majority out of the 1973 election had alerted everyone that the party intended to amend the constitution of the country and wanted to be in a position to do that without the need to solicit the support of the opposition parties in Parliament. There were many people not normally associated with the opposition parties who were afraid of the type of constitutional paring that would occur after the election. Perhaps to defuse these fears and to prevent these people from joining the ranks of the opposition, Burnham made the following declaration in a national radio broadcast four days before the 1973 election.

> The Constitution of Guyana, which was conceived and written with the full participation and agreement of the Party which I lead, proclaims Guyana as a democratic society founded upon the Rule of Law. As your Prime Minister, as Leader of the People's National Congress, and as a citizen, as an individual, I am totally committed, without reservation, to upholding the Constitution.[63]

Just over a year later, after the PNC had obtained two-thirds of the seats in Parliament and had weathered the protest over the conduct of the election, Forbes Burnham declared the constitution to be "out of step with modern trends, and our own ideas and ideologies; a Constitution which reflects for the most part the beliefs and ideology of our former imperialist masters."[64] In the same speech Burnham stated, "The drafting and promulgation of a new Constitution will, therefore, be undertaken shortly, that is from January 1975."[65]

The PNC was particularly interested in a strengthening of the power of the executive and in a diminution of the power of the legislative branch. There was, however, a major constitutional problem that the party had to confront. There were certain entrenched clauses, specified in Article 73 of the Constitution, each of which could only be changed if the change was approved by Parliament and by a majority vote in a national referendum.[66] The original purpose of these clauses was to protect certain basic freedoms and to prevent the exercise of absolute power by the executive branch. The PNC government chose to confront this problem in April 1978, three months before the life of the existing Parliament was due to end and six months before new elections were constitutionally required.

The PNC proposed to have one referendum in which it would ask the people to waive their right to be consulted on any future constitutional changes. The existing Parliament would then be converted into a Constituent Assembly to draft a new constitution. The enabling legislation, called the Constitution (Amendment) Bill No. 8 of 1978, was rushed through Parliament during the first few days of April, and the referendum date was set for July 10.[67] The PNC had no doubt that it would win the referendum, nor did anyone else.

However, protest was widespread and included opposition political parties, labor unions, professional and civic groups, and the churches. The Guyana Council of Churches opposed the bill on the ground that it placed too much power in the hands of any Parliament and too great a temptation for the existing Parliament or any future Parliaments to assume more power than was just.[68] A special committee of Guyana's lawyers condemned the bill as "an attempt to get the electorate to place a blank cheque on the national future in the hands of a spent Parliament."[69]

The PNC government demonstrated its contempt for the opposition, and indeed for the electorate, when it decided to assign a "house" as the symbol for a "yes" vote, and a "mouse" as the symbol for a "no" vote in the national referendum. The party slogan, painted prominently on the Georgetown sea wall was "Vote the House, Kill the Mouse."

Domestic groups, outside of the PNC party structure, were convinced that the referendum would not be fairly conducted. They decided to organize a national boycott of the referendum. Although the PNC used buses to shuffle supporters from one polling station to another, the boycott was very successful. Opposition groups estimated that between 10 and 15 percent of the electorate participated. However, the PNC claimed that there was a 71.45 percent turnout and that 97.4 percent of these voted for the "house."[70]

With the most restrictive clauses of Article 73 of the Constitution rendered inoperative by the outcome of the referendum, the PNC government used its two-thirds majority in Parliament to postpone, by 15 months, national elections that were constitutionally due no later than October 1978. Parliament was then converted into a Constituent Assembly and empowered with the rewriting of the constitution of the country. Although the PPP had helped to organize the boycott, the party decided to take up its seats in the new assembly. The PNC had already prepared a draft which was submitted to the Constituent Assembly. Other organizations were invited to submit their own drafts or to make recommendations, but few elected to do so. Protest against the rewriting of the constitution continued after the referendum. Nevertheless, the PNC persisted in the exercise and the final document was promulgated on October 6, 1980.

THE ASSASSINATION OF WALTER RODNEY

The WPA had been very active in organizing the boycott of the referendum in July 1978. It also acquired increased visibility after the Jonestown tragedy in November. There was a general clamor for an inquiry into the activities of the Reverend Jim Jones and the People's Temple and into all the circumstances that culminated in the bizarre death of 914 people. The PNC government resisted the institution of such an inquiry by dismissing the tragedy as an entirely American problem. In order to press the issue, opposition political parties, trade unions, civil rights groups, and social and cultural organizations established the

Council of National Safety and selected WPA's Kwayana as its secretary. The Council wanted a comprehensive inquiry into the Jonestown affair. The Council raised questions about the role of the PNC government in the affair. It wanted to know how the Jonestown commune acquired the type of autonomy that merited the classification of a "state within the state," and how the commune was able to circumvent Guyana's tough firearm regulations and acquire such a vast amount of arms and ammunition.[71] The Council of National Safety did not succeed in getting a comprehensive inquiry into the Jonestown affair, but its persistence kept domestic and regional interest focused on the issue. The government's inability or unwillingness to provide answers was interpreted by many as indicative of some level of complicity. The WPA's role in pressing the Jonestown issue gave the group increased political prominence.

The WPA drew considerable public sympathy and support when several of its leaders were charged with arson in July 1979. The WPA and the PPP had organized a week of protest beginning on July 10, the anniversary of the rigged referendum. The protest took the form of a candlelight vigil outside of the Parliament. Jagan took the first watch on July 10. A few hours after midnight, a fire gutted the building that housed the Ministry of National Development and the Office of the PNC General Secretary.[72] There was speculation that the fire had been purposely set by PNC activists. Nevertheless, the government arrested eight WPA officials including Walter Rodney and Professors Rupert Roopnaraine, Odle, and Omawale of the University of Guyana. On July 14, those arrested were released on bail. However, subsequent court proceedings, including the denial of a trial by jury, indicated that the government was intent on convicting these people.[73]

On July 20, six days after the WPA activists were released on bail, the WPA declared itself a political party. The party acknowledged no individual leader but claimed to be governed by an executive council of 14 people. There was no question that the party fielded an impressive array of leaders. Its public meetings drew large crowds. After the Gairy government in Grenada was overthrown in March 1979, Guyanese began to talk of a Grenada type of solution to the political problem in Guyana. The WPA was no doubt capitalizing on this general feeling when it dubbed 1979 "the Year of the Turn" against the PNC regime.[74] The WPA published its own proposals for a national patriotic front government in which it called for a democratic alliance of all political groups excluding the PNC. Burnham, on the other hand, tried to dismiss the WPA leaders as "the lunatic left" and described the party as the "Worst Possible Alternative."[75]

Walter Rodney became Burnham's tormentor, taunting Burnham in a fashion no other politician had been able to or dared to do. Burnham, who loved the name "Kabaka" or King was dubbed King Kong by

Rodney. The comical significance of the name was magnified by the fact that the Residence, Burnham's official home, is next door to the George-town zoo. In his July 20 speech, Rodney said, to the utter amusement of the crowd, "One of the brothers in the audience, when we were at Grove yesterday, suggested that what was required was to extend the zoo to take in the Residence and then we would have one of the most prize exhibits of any zoo in the world. People would come from all over the world and pay money to see King Kong."[76] In the same speech, Rodney assessed the performance of the Burnham regime thus: ". . . if there was such a thing called the Midas touch, which was the touch that made everything turn into gold, then we have a new creation in this society—the Burnham touch where everything he touches turns to shit. One has to put it in these brutal terms because the situation in which we are is a brutal situation."[77]

However, what transformed the political situation in Guyana in 1979 into an insurrectionary situation was the WPA's declared determination to remove the PNC by any means. As Rodney put it,

There is no way out under the present system. So we have got to make up our minds what we are deciding now within the Working People's Alliance. It is not simply that the government "do bad" and they must do better, it is not simply that they do part good and part bad and they must remedy it. It is not that they must reform. It is not that they must hold another election and rig it all up. We "finish" we all of that. *They must go! The P.N.C. Must Go!* And they must go by any means necessary.[78]

Burnham's reply came in August, in his address to the third biennial congress of the PNC. Burnham said, "The gauntlet has been thrown down. We have picked it up. The battle is joined. We ask no quarter and we shall give none. We shall use every weapon at our disposal. Let there be no weeping or complaints."[79] Within a year, Walter Rodney was dead.

The published evidence suggests that Rodney's death was the result of a conspiracy. On June 13, 1980, Walter Rodney was given a bomb disguised as a walkie-talkie by Gregory Smith, who was later identified as having connections with the Guyana Defense Force. The device exploded in his lap shortly afterwards killing Walter Rodney and injuring his younger brother, Donald, who was also present.[80] Although photographs of Gregory Smith were made public by some newspapers, no arrest was made. It is generally believed that Smith received official assistance in leaving the country. The U.S. Department of State Country Human Rights Report for 1980 addressed the question of Rodney's death as follows: "Available information indicates that the government was implicated in the June 13 death of WPA activist Walter Rodney and in the subsequent removal of key witnesses from the country."[81]

Rodney's gruesome assassination evoked enormous sympathy internally and internationally. Caribbean heads of state condemned the assassination. The funeral procession for Rodney took the form of a 12-mile trek on foot from Buxton-Annandale to Georgetown. Although it rained heavily on that day, the funeral procession attracted an estimated 35,000 people.[82]

The surviving WPA leaders pledged their determination to continue their struggle against the PNC regime.[83] However, privately, many were shocked by the manner of Rodney's death and concerned about their own safety. Excessive security precautions kept the WPA leaders indoors. They appeared unable to harness the sympathy and support that the party received following Rodney's death. In fact, the government took the offensive and embarked on a witchhunt against WPA supporters, particularly those in the teaching profession. Many were dismissed, while others were transferred to remote parts of the country almost assuring their resignations, since many could not make the move.[84] The WPA continued to function; but after Rodney, it was a tamer organization.

THE 1980 GENERAL ELECTION

On October 6, 1980, the new constitution was promulgated. The new constitution concentrated power in the Office of the Executive President. Forbes Burnham assumed the title of president without first facing an election. He did, however, set the date for the general election, which had been twice postponed, for December 15. In a radio broadcast Burnham said that he would have no objections to the presence of foreign observers during this election.

The opposition parties were convinced that the election would be rigged. Two parties—the WPA and the Vanguard for Liberation and Democracy—decided to boycott the elections. In fact, the WPA designated December 15 as a day of remembrance for Walter Rodney. The WPA and the Vanguard for Liberation and Democracy (VLD) called on the PPP to join the boycott. However, the PPP, along with the UF, decided to participate in the election in order to deprive the PNC of an excuse to set up a one-party state.[85] Many suspected that the PPP's motives were much more selfish. Like the ruling PNC, the PPP was astonished by the popularity of the WPA. By participating in the election the party could be assured of a number of seats in Parliament and the PPP leader would retain the official title of Leader of the Opposition.

Nevertheless, the opposition parties invited an international team of observers to witness the conduct of the election. The team was headed by Lord Avebury, Secretary of the British Parliamentary Human Rights Group, and included representatives from the Canadian Council of

Churches, the Caribbean Council of Churches, the Lutheran Church of North America, and the Vatican observer to the Organization of American States.[86]

The team arrived in Guyana on December 9. They witnessed some of the pre-election campaigning and were present for the election on December 15. They alleged that the government interfered with their work. The head of the team, Lord Avebury, was detained by the police on election day. The team observed that the entire polling process was in the hands of PNC supporters. Commenting on some of the irregularities on election day, the team's report stated:

We have massive evidence that large numbers of eligible voters were denied their right to vote. The following are examples: deletion of names from the electoral list; abuse of proxy voting; abuse of postal voting; people were told that they were dead; PNC agents outside the polls gave people slips of paper bearing wrong ID numbers, or told them their names were not on the list, although they were; voters were disenfranchised because of minor technical or clerical errors in the list; fraudulent votes had already been cast in the voters', name; evidence was supplied to us of double registration. These abuses were primarily directed against supporters of the opposition parties.[87]

When the results were announced the PNC won 78 percent of the votes cast and 41 of the 53 parliamentary seats. The PPP received 19 percent of the votes cast and 10 parliamentary seats, and the UF won 2 seats with 3 percent of the votes. The international team of observers ended their report with the following lamentation:

We came to Guyana aware of the serious doubts expressed about the conduct of previous elections there, but determined to judge these elections on their own merit and hoping to be able to say that the result was fair. We deeply regret that, on the contrary, we were obliged to conclude, on the basis of abundant and clear evidence that the election was rigged massively and flagrantly. Fortunately, however, the scale of the fraud made it impossible to conceal either from the Guyanese public or the outside world. Far from legitimizing President Burnham's assumption of his office, the events we witnessed confirm all the fears of Guyanese and foreign observers about the state of democracy in that country.

Lady Guymine, a famous local calypso artist, sang at the time: "The elections in Guyana will be something to remember." Sadly, they were, as an example of the way an individual's determination to cling to power at all costs can poison the springs of democracy.[88]

A REPEAT PERFORMANCE

Deteriorating social and economic conditions in the country motivated the Guyana Council of Churches in 1982 to convene a conference of political parties, trade unions, religious and social organizations. The sponsors hoped that a creative and united solution would emerge from the talks. The talks began on April 7 and lasted through December. All of the political parties, except the PNC, attended the talks. The parties agreed on the need for a broad-based democratic government but could not come up with a program to bring this about. The WPA hoped that the talks would yield a program of political action to remove the PNC from power and to install a caretaker government with a "minimum programme," pending national elections under the provisions of the 1966 constitution. The PPP took the position that a broad-based democratic government must include the PNC which the PPP saw as a "progressive" party. The PPP was insistent that any broad-based government must be based on "revolutionary democracy," "anti-imperialism," and "socialist orientation." Nothing tangible came out of the talks. The PPP, however, was able to monitor the talks and to use these to communicate conciliatory signals to the PNC.[89]

In 1985, Guyana was awash with rumors of a possible PNC-PPP coalition. The PNC had invited the PPP to engage in a "constructive dialogue."[90] It was the first time ever that the PNC had initiated these types of talks with the PPP. The scheduling of the talks had been at the urging of the Cuban government, but the Burnham regime was in a desperate position and needed the collaboration of the PPP. The economy was in shambles, foreign aid sources had dried up, and exhortations for greater productivity went unheeded by the general population. Faced with these circumstances, Burnham may have felt that some concessions to the PPP might create an appearance of national unity and inspire the populace to greater productivity.

The Burnham-Jagan talks had a tremendous impact on the WPA. Prior to the talks, WPA had renounced the use of violence as a mechanism for changing the government. This was the prudent thing to do since the WPA activists had been the subjects of numerous arms searches and had been singled out for other forms of harassment. Now the WPA also changed its position on the question of a national front government. Until 1985, the WPA had supported the PPP's call for a national front government, but was insistent on the exclusion of the PNC. The Burnham-Jagan talks no doubt made the WPA fearful of being left out of a political solution. As a result, it changed its position with regard to the PNC. It declared its support for a national front government that included all major political parties in the country, including the PNC.[91]

The talks between Burnham and Jagan continued until Burnham's death in August. Burnham's successor, Desmond Hoyte, agreed to continue the talks.[92] However, Hoyte proceeded to name a date for the next national election whereupon the PPP and the other parties began to seek assurances of a free and fair election. The adversarial relationship between the PNC and the PPP reasserted itself and completely overshadowed the "constructive dialogue."

Elections, later described by the *Catholic Standard* as "the most flagrantly rigged Elections in the history of Guyana," took place on December 9, 1985.[93] Six political parties took the field against the PNC. Apart from the PPP, WPA, and UF, there were the People's Democratic Movement (PDM), and two newer parties, the Democratic Labor Movement (DLM), and the National Democratic Front (NDF). The Liberator Party had ceased to exist when its leader, Ganraj Kumar, retired from politics in 1984. The opposition parties had hoped that Hoyte might break with past PNC cheating and hold a fair election. This proved to be a false hope. The 1985 elections were conducted in a similar fashion to those of 1980. Indeed, many Guyanese were cynically commenting that Forbes Burnham had already compiled the election results before he died in August.

In preparation for the elections, the PNC government reenacted Part II of the National Security Act, which gave the security forces wider detention powers including the power to prevent someone "from acting in a manner likely to cause subversion of democratic institutions in Guyana."[94] The discretionary nature of this latter provision added to the intimidating effect of this measure on supporters of the opposition parties. Further, the announcement by Major General McLean that the army would secure and escort the ballot boxes resurrected grim memories of the army quarantining and sanitizing the ballot boxes.[95]

The election results were not announced until December 12, three days after balloting was over. The PNC obtained 42 seats, the PPP received 8, the United Force received 2, and the WPA received 1 seat.[96] However, a joint statement by a number of civic groups, including the Guyana Bar Association, the Anglican Church, and the Catholic Church, condemned "the familiar and sordid catalogue of widespread disenfranchisement, multiple voting, ejection of polling agents, violence and collusion by police and army personnel."[97] President Hoyte had demonstrated his intention to continue the practice of electoral fraud that has kept the PNC in power and allowed it to elude accountability.

NOTES

1. 98th Congress, 2nd Session, Joint Committee Print: *Country Reports on Human Rights Practices for 1983: Report submitted to the Committee on Foreign Affairs, U.S. House of Representatives and the Committee on Foreign Relations, U.S. Senate by the Department of State in Accordance with Sections 116(d) and 502(b) of the Foreign Assistance Act of 1961 as Amended February 1984* (Washington, D.C.: U.S. Government Printing Office, 1984), p. 593.

2. Halperin, "Racism and Communism," pp. 127–128.

3. Jagan, *The West on Trial*, p. 321.

4. Spinner, *A Political and Social History*, p. 122.

5. J. E. Greene, *Race vs. Politics in Guyana* (Kingston: Institute of Social and Economic Research, University of the West Indies, 1974), p. 28.

6. *Ibid.*, p. 29. See also People's Progressive Party, *Rigged Elections in Guyana* (Ruimveldt: New Guyana Company Limited, 1978), pp. 30–44.

7. Figures taken from Greene, *Race vs. Politics in Guyana*, p. 28.

8. Spinner, *A Political and Social History*, p. 128.

9. Jagan, *The West on Trial*, p. 323; Greene, *Race vs. Politics in Guyana*, pp. 29–30.

10. Greene, *Race vs. Politics in Guyana*, pp. 29–30.

11. *Ibid.*, p. 30; People's Progressive Party, *Rigged Elections in Guyana*, p. 36.

12. People's Progressive Party, *Rigged Elections in Guyana*, p. 38.

13. Greene, *Race vs. Politics in Guyana*, p. 29.

14. This became common knowledge among the farmers in Black Bush Polder on the Corentyne coast.

15. People's Progressive Party, *Rigged Elections in Guyana*, p. 66.

16. The proxy collectors in each electoral district became very well known.

17. Spinner, *A Political and Social History*, p. 146.

18. *Ibid.*

19. People's Progressive Party, *Rigged Elections in Guyana*, p. 18.

20. Cited in People's Progressive Party, *Rigged Elections in Guyana*, p. 66.

21. Walter Rodney, *The Struggle Goes On!* (Georgetown: WPA, 1979), p. 8.

22. Forbes Burnham, "A Vision of the Co-operative Republic," in L. Searwar, ed. *Co-operative Republic Guyana 1970: A Study of Aspects of our Way of Life* (Georgetown: The Government of Guyana, 1970), p. 10.

23. Nascimento and Burrowes, eds., *A Destiny to Mould*, p. 157.

24. People's National Congress, *Policy Paper: Co-operatism* (Georgetown: Guyana National Lithographic Co. Ltd., no date), p. 13.

25. *Ibid.*, pp. 29–39. See also, Forbes Burnham, *Towards the Socialist Revolution* (Georgetown: Guyana Printers Ltd., 1975), p. 29; Forbes Burnham, *Economic Liberation Through Socialism* (Georgetown: Guyana Printers Ltd., 1977), pp. 15–19.

26. Forbes Burnham, *Declaration of Sophia* (Georgetown: Guyana Printers Ltd., 1974), p. 9.

27. Greene, *Race vs. Politics in Guyana*, p. 45. See also Robert H. Manley, *Guyana Emergent*, pp. 107–109.

28. Ali A. Mazrui and Michael Tidy, *Nationalism and New States in Africa* (Portsmouth: Heinemann Educational Books, Inc., 1985), pp. 295–296; Joseph Weatherby, Jr., et al., *The Other World: Issues and Politics in the Third World* (New York: Macmillan Publishing Company, 1987), pp. 175–176.

29. Cheddi Jagan, "Report of the Central Committee to the 19th Congress of the PPP," in *Documents of the 19th Congress, People's Progressive Party* (Georgetown: The New Guyana Company, Ltd., 1976), p. 48.

30. James A. Sackey, "Dependence, Underdevelopment and Socialist-Oriented Transformation in Guyana," *Inter-American Economic Affairs* 33 (Summer 1979), pp. 40–42.

31. R. S. Milne, "Guyana's Cooperative Republic," *Parliamentary Affairs* 27 (Autumn 1975), pp. 353–354.

32. Ralph R. Premdas, "Guyana: Communal Conflict, Socialism and Political Reconciliation," *Inter-American Economic Affairs* 30 (Spring 1977), pp. 70–71.

33. The only other radio station, the Guyana Broadcasting Station (GBS), was already under government control. Guyana has no television.

34. Ralph R. Premdas, "Guyana: Socialist Reconstruction . . . ," p. 136. See also Anthony P. Maingot, "The Difficult Path to Socialism in the English-Speaking Caribbean," in Richard R. Fagen, ed., *The State in United States—Latin American Relations* (Stanford, CA: Stanford University Press, 1979), p. 269.

35. Forbes Burnham, *Economic Liberation Through Socialism* (Ruimveldt: Guyana Printers Ltd., 1977), p. 15.

36. Forbes Burnham, *Towards the Socialist Revolution* (Ruimveldt: Guyana Printers Ltd., 1975), pp. 5–6.

37. People's National Congress, *Policy Paper: Co-operatism*, pp. 57–59.

38. Forbes Burnham, *Economic Liberation Through Socialism*, p. 10.

39. *Ibid*.

40. The PNC promulgated a new constitution on October 6, 1980 that provided for an executive president. See Chapter 4 of this book.

41. "Burnham's New Appointments," *Caribbean Contact* (September 1984), p. 2; "President Hoyte, PM Greene—A Study in Contrasts," *Caribbean Contact* (September 1985), p. 9.

42. "Power struggle looks likely after Forbes Burnham's death," *Latin America Weekly Report* (August 16, 1985), p. 1; "Guyana: 'High hopes' on US help," *Latin America Weekly Report* (June 26, 1986), p. 3.

43. "Cde Viola Burnham New Vice-President, Dep. Prime Minister," *Sunday Chronicle* (August 18, 1985), p. 1.

44. Simms, *Trouble in Guyana*, pp . 176–182.

45. Maingot, "The Difficult Path to Socialism. . .," p. 263.

46. Jagan, *The West on Trial*, p. 419.

47. Premdas, "Guyana: Communal Conflict. . .," pp. 72–74.

48. Rickey Singh, "Politics of Two Men in a Divided Land," *Caribbean Contact* (September 1975), p. 5; Hubert Williams, "PPP's Return to Parliament—A Possible National Govt?" *Caribbean Contact* (April 1976), p. 7.

49. Cited in Premdas, "Guyana: Socialist Reconstruction . . . ," 1978, p. 136.

50. Cheddi Jagan, "Report of the Central Committee to the 19th Congress of the PPP, in *Documents of the 19th Congress, People's Progressive Party* (Georgetown: the New Guyana Company Ltd., 1976), p. 38.

51. Clinton Collymore, *This is Guyana* (Ruimveldt: New Guyana Company Ltd., 1977), p. 24.

52. Premdas, "Guyana: Communal Conflict. . .," p. 74.

53. Jagan, "Report of the Central Committee . . . ," pp. 49–52.

54. "Government Charged With Cover-up Over Minister's Death," *Catholic Standard*, November 11, 1979, p. 1.

55. "For a National Front Government," Central Committee Document, People's Progressive Party, August 1977, pp. 30–31.

56. Hubert Williams, "Confrontation Politics in Guyana: Police Hunting Kwayana," *Caribbean Contact* (November 1976), p. 9.

57. Jagan, "Report of the Central Committee . . . ," p. 28.

58. *Ibid.*, p. 29; Eusi Kwayana, *Walter Rodney* (Georgetown: Working People's Alliance, 1986), pp. 5–7.

59. Kwayana, *Walter Rodney*, p. 9.

60. *Ibid.*, p. 12; see also Hubert Williams, "Targets of Strike by Guybau's Workers," *Caribbean Contact* (January 1977), p. 20.

61. Kwayana, *Walter Rodney*, p. 8.

62. The author of this book was one of the teachers affected. Fr. Malcolm Rodrigues, S.J., "Dismissal of Teacher from C.H.S. Questioned," *Catholic Standard*, January 16, 1977, p. 1; "Unexplained Dismissal Sparks 2-week strike at C.H.S.," *Catholic Standard*, January 23, 1977, p. 1; Lionel Ramjeet, "School Heads Appeal: End Boycott Now," *Guyana Chronicle*, February 1, 1977, p. 1; Kwayana, *Walter Rodney*. p. 14.

63. Forbes Burnham, "Investment for the Future," in *Four Talks to the Nation: 1973 Election Addresses to the Nation by the Honourable L. F. S. Burnham O. E., S. C., Prime Minister, Guyana, South America* (No additional publication information), p. 12.

64. Forbes Burnham, *Declaration of Sophia*, p. 19.

65. *Ibid.*

66. "Die is Cast in Guyana's Constitution Political Battle," *Caribbean Contact* (June 1978), pp. 8–9; *The Laws of Guyana: The Constitution* (Georgetown: Guyana Lithographic Co. Ltd., 1973), p. 62.

67. "July 10 Referendum: Towards Absolute Power in Guyana," *Caribbean Contact* (July 1978), p. 5.

68. "Why Local Churches Oppose," *Caribbean Contact* (June 1978), p. 9.

69. "The Lawyers' Case Against Bill," *Carribean Contact* (June 1978), p. 9.

70. Spinner, *A Political and Social History*, p. 166.

71. "Guyana Through the Eyes of the National Safety Council," *Caribbean Contact* (March 1979), p. 13. See also "Temple Massacre Could Have Been Stopped," *Caribbean Contact* (December 1978), pp. 1–8.

72. "Guyana: Trial of the 'Referendum Five'," *Africa* (September 1979), pp. 95–96; Kwayana, *Walter Rodney*, pp. 21–24.

73. For some of the proceedings of the trial, see Spinner, *A Political and Social History*, pp. 181–182.

74. "Rodney Tells Why PNC Panicking in This 'Year of the Turn'," *Caribbean Contact* (September 1979), p. 12.

75. Forbes Burnham, *Towards the People's Victory*: (Ruimveldt: Guyana Printers Ltd., 1979), p. 20; *National Unity for Democracy, Peace and Social Progress: Report of the Central Committee to the 22nd Congress of the People's Progressive Party* (Annandale: People's Progressive Party, 1985), p. 93.

76. Walter Rodney, *The Struggle Goes On!* (Georgetown: WPA, 1979), p. 6.

77. *Ibid.*, p. 7.

78. *Ibid.*, p. 15.

79. Burnham, *Towards the People's Victory*, p. 26.

80. Rickey Singh, "Guyana's Sensational Murder," *Caribbean Contact* (July 1980), p. 1.

81. 97th Congress, 1st Session, Joint Committee Print, *Country Reports on Human Rights Practices: Report Submitted to the Committee on Foreign Relations, U.S.*

Senate and Committee on Foreign Affairs U.S. House of Representatives by the Department of State in Accordance with Sections 116(d) and 502 (b) of the Foreign Assistance Act of 1961 as Amended February 2, 1981 (Washington, D.C.: U.S. Government Printing Office, 1984), p. 456.

82. Singh, "Guyana's Sensational Murder," pp. 1, 16.

83. Dr. Rupert Roopnarain, "WPA Tells of the Way Forward," *Caribbean Contact* (July 1980), pp. 10–11.

84. Guyana Human Rights Association, *Human Rights Report, Jan. 1980-June 1981* (Georgetown: Guyana Human Rights Association, 1981), pp. 39–43.

85. "Guyana Elections and Boycott Call," *Caribbean Contact* (December 1980), p. 1.

86. Lord Avebury and the British Parliamentary Human Rights Group, "Guyana's 1980 Elections: The Politics of Fraud," *Caribbean Review* 10 (Spring 1981), p. 10.

87. *Ibid.*, p. 44.

88. *Ibid.*, p. 44.

89. Working People's Alliance, *Arguments For Unity Against The Dictatorship in Guyana* (Georgetown: Working People's Alliance, 1983), pp. 1–12; see also *National Unity for Democracy. . . ,* pp. 69–102.

90. "Rumours of PNC/PPP Coalition Divert Guyanese," *Caribbean Contact* (March 1985), p. 2.

91. "What Purpose/Role For WPA in Guyana?" *Caribbean Contact* (May 1985), p. 10; "WPA Makes Its Case," *Caribbean Contact* (June 1985), p. 10.

92. "PNC-PPP Talks Are Still On," *Latin America Weekly Report* (August 30, 1985), p. 5.

93. "Massive Fraud As PNC Imposes Self Rule," *Catholic Standard* (December 15, 1985), p. 1.

94. "Bill Tabled to Re-enact National Security Act," *Catholic Standard* (June 9, 1985), p. 1.

95. "Spectre Looms Of Army Involvement," *Mirror* (October 20, 1985), p. 1.

96. These results were provided by the Embassy of Guyana, Washington, D.C.

97. "An Absurdity?" *Caribbean Contact* (January 1986), p. 5.

4

POLITICAL INSTITUTIONS

INTRODUCTION

The constitution that Guyana received at its independence was a blue-print for a liberal democracy. Unfortunately, the PNC began to see many of the constitutional provisions as obstacles to its consolidation of state power and eventually decided to overhaul the entire document. The end result was the creation of an executive president with the powers of a Seventeenth century French monarch. However, increased executive power did not result in greater compliance by the Guyanese public, and while electoral malpractices may have allowed the PNC to retain political power, they also made the party uncertain about the strength of support it really had. Further, with church groups, civic groups, and labor unions joining the opposition parties in criticizing the PNC, the party became obsessed with the need to control its opponents. To this end, the regime resorted to intimidation, a major element of which consisted of creating the appearance of an ethnic confrontation between blacks and Indians and then trying to get blacks to see the PNC as their protector. The strategy was foiled by the WPA, but it exposed Indian rural communities to some of the worst crimes in the country's history.

THE INDEPENDENCE CONSTITUTION

Guyana became independent on May 26, 1966, and on that day a new constitution was promulgated. It was a very elaborate document, about ten times the length of the United States Constitution. It was conceived and written with the full consent of the PNC. Even the PPP, which had boycotted the constitutional conference that produced this document, did not find fault with this constitution.

The constitution provided that Guyana would be a democratic, unitary state within the British Commonwealth. The Queen of the United King-dom remained the titular head of state and was represented in Guyana by the governor-general, who was to be the commander-in-chief of the armed forces. However, Article 73 of the Constitution provided for Guyana to become a republic if the prime minister introduced a motion to that effect in the national assembly and if it was supported by a majority. The only stipulation was that the change could not occur before April 4, 1969. On August 26, 1969, such a motion was passed to make Guyana a republic on February 23, 1970. The date was chosen to commemorate the 1763 Berbice slave revolt led by Guyana's national hero, Cuffy. The position of governor-general was eliminated, and in its place the position of president of the republic was created. The president was to be the ceremonial head of state and commander-in-chief of the armed forces of Guyana. The term of office was set at six years and election was to be by secret ballot of the members of Parliament.[1] The only person to be elected to the office of president under this constitution was Arthur Chung, a high court judge. Chung is Chinese, a factor that featured significantly in his selection. It was felt that, given Guyana's racial structure, an Afro-Guyanese or an Indian in that position would not be able to command the affection or allegiance of the other major ethnic group. As it turned out, Chung commanded little respect, affection, or allegiance. He had no political following. A very diminutive man with very little personal presence, Chung appeared awkward in official dress, particularly in military uniform which he apparently felt he ought to wear as commander-in-chief of the armed forces. He was reelected for a second term in 1976. However, he did not serve out this term since the post was eliminated in 1980.

The independence constitution provided for a cabinet government similar to that of Great Britain. The actual locus of executive power resided in the office of the prime minister. The prime minister was to be the elected member of the legislature who could command the support of the majority of the elected members in that body, in effect the leader of the party winning a majority of the legislative seats in the general election. The prime minister would then appoint the other ministers of the cabinet, who did not have to be elected members of the legislature.[2] With a legislative majority, the prime minister's party would not have any difficulty enacting its program.

The constitution provided for the establishment of a unicameral parliament consisting of 53 elected members. The election of members of Parliament was to be by secret ballot in accordance with the system of proportional representation. Each political party would submit a list of candidates, and votes would be cast for the entire list, in effect, for the party. The 53 seats would then be allocated among the parties in direct proportion to the votes polled by each party. The term of Parliament was set at five years, though the prime minister could call a general election earlier.[3] Except for the system of election and for the absence of an upper house in the Parliament, the Guyanese system of government was modeled after the British system.

As a check on possible abuse of governmental power, the constitution provided for the appointment of an ombudsman. Forbes Burnham had been particularly insistent on the inclusion of this office in the constitution. At the opening session of the 1965 Constitutional Conference at Lancaster House, London, on November 2, 1965, he stated: "We also want to see in the constitution coming out of this conference, the institution of the Office of Ombudsman, the holder of which will have statutory authority to investigate complaints of discrimination and irregular use of State-power, and to take the necessary action in terms of the spirit of the constitution and the public interest."[4] As provided by the constitution, the ombudsman could, on the basis of citizen or group complaint, investigate the actions taken by any official or any department of government. He could then make recommendations for the redress of grievances. If no action was taken within a reasonable time, the ombudsman could then present a special report on the case to the Parliament.[5] The inclusion of an ombudsman in the constitution seemed to be an added guarantee of a functioning democracy. However, the practice varied considerably from the design. The first ombudsman, Gordon Gillette, resigned in frustration. It was generally believed that the government was not cooperating with him, if not obstructing the work of his office. The position has since been filled with a political appointee and the importance of the office has been downgraded.

The judicial system established by the independence constitution was merely a modification of the one in operation until 1966. The magistrate's court remained as the lowest court. The Supreme Court in existence before 1966 became the High Court. Any appeal from the High Court was to be heard by the Court of Appeal. There was, however, provision for appeal beyond Guyana's Court of Appeal. Such an appeal would be heard by the Judicial Committee of the British Privy Council.[6] This latter practice was discontinued after Guyana became a republic in 1970.

The independence constitution also created several semiautonomous public commissions that were meant to function in an independent and impartial manner. These commissions were the Judicial Service Commission, the Public Service Commission, the Police Service Commission, and the Elections Commission. Of these the Elections Commission was the first to succumb to state power. The key functions assigned by the constitution to the Elections Commission were the registration of electors and the conduct of elections.[7] In 1968, the Burnham government took control over these functions and assigned them to the Ministry of Home Affairs. Since that time, the Elections Commission became an instrument of the ruling party and has been used to certify the results of elections that are carefully managed by the PNC. The party also subverted the independence of the other public commissions.

THE PARAMOUNTCY OF THE PARTY

In 1974, the PNC leadership began a doctrinal offensive to make the party the dominant institution in Guyanese society. In his "Declaration of Sophia" address, given at a special congress to mark the tenth anniversary of the PNC in government, Burnham enunciated the doctrine of the paramountcy of the party. He declared that *"the Party should assume unapologetically its paramountcy over the Government which is merely one of its executive arms.* The comrades demanded that the country be given practical and theoretical leadership at all levels—political, economic, social and cultural—by the PNC which had become the major national institution"[8] (emphasis added). With this declaration Burnham was staking out for the PNC the hegemonic role that socialist parties enjoy in Eastern bloc countries. This doctrine formally signified the end of liberal democracy in Guyana. It also implied that as "the major national institution," the PNC could not be replaced, at least not by constitutional means.

The paramountcy doctrine and the provisions of the PNC party constitution positioned the party leader to exercise absolute power. According to Article 21 of the PNC Party Constitution,

If the leader, in his deliberate judgements is of the opinion that a situation of emergency has arisen in the Party, he shall have the power notwithstanding any provision in these rules, on giving notice to the General Secretary of his opinion, to take all action that he may *in his absolute discretion* consider necessary to correct such a situation; and for this purpose *he may assume and exercise any and all of the powers of the Biennial Delegates' Congress, the General Council, the Central Executive Committee, any other Committee, Group, Arm, Organ or any officer or official of the Party*[9] (emphasis added).

This rule gives the party leader absolute control over the party, and if the party is paramount over all state institutions, then it follows that the PNC leader is also paramount over all state institutions.

The PNC utilized a variety of mechanisms to implement the doctrine of party paramountcy. Within the government, it created a new ministry that merged the Office of the General Secretary of the PNC with the Ministry of National Development. This move permitted the ruling party to use public funds to support the activities of the party. The annual expenditures of this new department varies between G$8 million and G$10 million, the bulk of which is classified as "miscellaneous expenditures." Between 1975 and 1980, G$54.3 million were allocated to this department. However, only G$1.4 million have been accounted for, suggesting that the paramountcy principle frees the government of accountability to any but the party.[10] In other words, the blurring of the distinction between the party and the government allows the party to steal public funds.

The paramountcy principle was also implemented by a redefinition of the role of the security forces. According to the independence constitution, President Chung was the commander-in-chief of the armed forces of Guyana. However, Forbes Burnham, in addition to being prime minister, kept the portfolio of minister of defense from which he exercised strong control over the armed forces. At the first biennial congress of the PNC in 1975, the military and para-military forces were required by Burnham to pledge their allegiance to the PNC.[11] Burnham subsequently appeared in public in military uniform, displaying the insignia of a general. Guyana had no other generals at the time, so that Burnham outranked all of the officers of the Guyana Defense Force. Burnham also appeared in public in the uniforms of the para-military forces, and in each case, his uniform bore the insignia of the highest rank. It was clear that Burnham was exercising the powers of commander-in-chief of the armed forces, powers that by the constitution belonged to President Chung. Chung's status was further downgraded when the PNC decided to address him as "comrade," a form of appellation hitherto reserved for party functionaries.

To further emphasize the dominance of the ruling party over state institutions, the PNC flag was flown over the Court of Appeal.[12] This undermined public confidence in the judicial system since it suggested that the court was subservient to the party. In fact, the PNC began to use the courts as part of the machinery to intimidate individuals as well as organizations that were identified as opponents of the ruling party.

Thus, although the independence constitution provided the framework for a liberal democracy, the essence of the state in Guyana in the 1970s was authoritarian, and there was no question that all the strands of power converged on the person of Forbes Burnham. In 1978, Burnham moved to formalize his powers by overhauling the constitution.

THE SOCIALIST CONSTITUTION

Guyana's new constitution, called the socialist constitution, was promulgated on October 6, 1980. It is a very elaborate document: 135 pages long. The ideology underlying the constitution is a socialist one. In the preamble to the constitution, which is over ten times the length of the preamble to the U.S. Constitution, the framers attest to the belief that the organization of the state and society on socialist principles is the only way to ensure social and economic justice for all Guyanese. Article

1 describes Guyana as "an indivisible, secular, democratic sovereign state in the course of transition from capitalism to socialism,"[13] which suggests that another constitution can be anticipated when Guyana is adjudged to have reached the stage of socialism. Articles 15 and 16 announce the intention of the state to revolutionize the economy and to use the principles of cooperativism to achieve the socialist transformation of the society.[14] Barring these socialist declarations, the most significant aspect of the new constitution is the reconfiguration of state power to locate and consolidate absolute power in the office of an executive president.

The socialist constitution declares that there would be five "supreme organs of democratic power in Guyana." These are: (1) the National Congress of Local Democratic Organs; (2) the Parliament; (3) the Supreme Congress of the People; (4) the President; and (5) the Cabinet.[15] The "local democratic organs" are organizationally patterned after the Committees for the Defense of the Revolution in Cuba. For the purpose of organizing these local democratic organs, Guyana is divided into ten regions. Each region will have a regional council, the members of which will be elected by the people residing in that region. Each region is to be subdivided into an unspecified number of units and each of these subdivisions will have one local democratic organ. The constitution provides for the establishment of a National Congress of Local Government Organs, whose members will be elected by and from among the members of the local democratic organs. The responsibility of this organization is defined as representing the interests of local government in Guyana.[16]

Under the new constitution, the number of members of Parliament has been extended to 65. As before, 53 members are to be elected nationwide on the basis of proportional representation. Now, however, one member is selected from each of the ten regional councils and two members are elected from the members of the National Congress of Local Democratic Organs. However, the new Parliament is a much paler version of the Parliament under the independence constitution because the new constitution gives to the president the power to dissolve Parliament by proclamation, entirely at his discretion.[17]

The socialist constitution also provides for the establishment of a Supreme Congress of the People, consisting of all the members of Parliament and all the members of the National Congress of Local Democratic Organs. According to the constitution, the Supreme Congress will meet at places and times designated by the president and will make recommendations on matters of public interest referred to it by the president. The president may dissolve the Supreme Congress at any time, by proclamation.[18]

The most powerful of the five "Supreme Organs of Democratic Power" is the president. The president is the "Head of State, the supreme executive authority, and commander-in-chief of the armed forces of the Republic."[19] The president can veto any piece of legislation passed by Parliament. If two-thirds of the elected members of Parliament resolve that the bill should be presented again to the president for assent, "the President shall assent to it within twenty-one days of its presentation, *unless he sooner dissolves Parliament*"[20] (emphasis added). The president is immune from prosecution for anything done by him in his official or private capacity. The constitution has a provision for the removal of the president if he violates the constitution or if he engages in gross misconduct. However, this is really a pseudoprovision. A resolution to remove the president must be supported by not less than three-quarters of all elected members of the Parliament and "if the Assembly so resolves, the president shall cease to hold office upon the third day following the passage of the resolution *unless he sooner dissolves Parliament*"[21] (emphasis added).

The president is elected in the same manner as the other members of Parliament. When each party submits its list of candidates for the general election, it designates a presidential candidate. The slate of candidates that wins the most votes will have its designee become president.

The socialist constitution provides for a cabinet consisting of the president, the prime minister, the vice-presidents, and the other ministers appointed by the president. The prime minister must be an elected member of Parliament, and the constitution describes him as "the principal assistant of the President in the discharge of his executive functions and leader of Government business in the National Assembly."[22] In effect, while the president predominates in every domain of governmental activity, the prime minister implements his decisions and defends these in Parliament. The president may, for the purpose of assisting him in the discharge of his duties, appoint as many vice-presidents as he wishes. The prime minister is also a vice-president and is granted precedence over all other vice-presidents. With the exception of the prime minister, the vice-presidents and other ministers appointed by the president do not have to be members of Parliament.

The socialist constitution retains the office of ombudsman. However, given the low regard with which this position is generally held, the retention of this position seems to be only as a constitutional nicety intended to deflect attention from the consolidation of power in the office of president. Besides, as a high-paying position, it has patronage potential.

The socialist constitution unquestionably confers imperial powers on the holder of the office of president. On October 6, 1980, without first facing an election, Forbes Burnham simply assumed the title of president. It is interesting to note that throughout his political career, Burnham was fond of calling himself the "Kabaka," which in Swahili means the "King." With the promulgation of this new constitution and with his assumption of the title of president, Burnham finally succeeded in crowning himself.

THE SECURITY FORCES

The new constitution may have provided the legal basis for the authoritarian superstructure created by the PNC. However, what provide the buttress for this structure and defend it from groups demanding more democratic government are the security forces. The PNC regime maintains a very elaborate structure of military and para-military forces, particularly in comparison with the size of the population. A conservative estimate of these forces would put the total at 21,000 armed personnel. This means that there is one armed person for every 38 citizens. The PNC has justified the retention of such huge forces by reference to the border problem that the country has with Venezuela. However, Guyana's efforts in resisting the Venezuelan territorial claim have been focused at the diplomatic level. The troops deployed along the border are a small fraction of the total and are meant to assert Guyanese sovereignty and to monitor Venezuelan troop movements. The principal use of the military and para-military forces is in internal security. It is for this reason that these forces are required to publicly pledge allegiance to the PNC.

The Guyana Defense Force

The principal component of the security forces is the army whose official title is the Guyana Defense Force (GDF). Guyana does not have an air force or a navy. There is a small air wing with ten light aircraft and six helicopters, and a marine wing with eight coastal patrol vessels. Both of these fall within the GDF's organization and control. The GDF has a total strength of 7,000 armed personnel.[23]

The GDF started out as a constabulary force called the Special Service Unit (SSU). The SSU was created in 1964 by Governor Richard Luyt to aid the police force in maintaining internal order, but there was also the understanding that the SSU would become the country's army after independence was attained. The organization and training of the SSU was assigned to a British officer, Colonel Ronald Pope, and the British also provided a military training cadre. The Guyanese component of the commissioned officer corps and the noncommissioned officer corps was drawn from the Volunteer Force, a reservist unit consisting almost entirely of black civil servants. However officer cadets were also being selected outside of the Volunteer Force, for training in Britain. Through accelerated promotions, the Guyanese officers were being positioned to take over command from the British after independence.

Because the police force was predominantly black and because of the ethnic problems facing the country in the early 1960s, the British governor made a conscious effort to achieve an ethnic balance in the SSU. This was particularly evident in the selection of the cadets who were to fill the junior ranks of the officer corps. Indians were very well represented among the candidates selected to be trained at the Mons Officer Cadet Training School in England.

In 1965, the SSU underwent a name change to become the Guyana Defense Force. After independence in 1966, the transition began toward complete control of the GDF by Guyanese officers. The entire process took place under the scrutiny of Forbes Burnham, who, in addition to being prime minister, was also the minister of defense. The choice of the first Guyanese officer for the position of force commander gave a glimpse of what would later become a pattern in the army. The heir apparent to Colonel Pope, the British officer, was Major Raymond Sattaur, an Indian officer who had been trained at the Royal Military Academy at Sandhurst. Ethnic considerations appear to have been paramount in Burnham's decision to bypass Sattaur and to appoint Major Clarence Price, a black officer, formerly with the reservist Volunteer Force. After the 1968 election, when Burnham acquired firmer control over the government, he began to purge the officer corps of non-Africans. By 1970, the GDF had become predominantly black, both in the enlisted ranks and in the officer corps. The practice of sending officer cadets to Britain for training was terminated. A six-month cadet course was set up locally at the Timehri base. This allowed the PNC to be more politically selective of new entrants into the officer corps. Educational requirements were deemphasized, and political affiliation became the key criterion for selection. The overwhelming number of entrants have been blacks.

After independence, the PNC attempted to secure and maintain the loyalty of the GDF by manipulating racial symbols and by lavishing the officers with material benefits. The PNC portrayed itself as the only party capable of protecting black interests. The PPP, on the other hand, was portrayed as an Indian party whose victory at the polls would usher in an era of Indian economic and political domination of blacks. This was the approach used by the PNC to secure black support generally in Guyana. However, within the GDF, the message was transmitted by the more politically-minded officers. In 1973, the chief "political" officer in the GDF was Major David Granger, an aide to Forbes Burnham.[24] Granger openly advocated that the GDF should pledge its allegiance to the PNC. This position was not universally shared within the officer corps, but the more professionally-minded officers were prudent enough not to voice their disagreement openly. In any case, silence seemed to be a small price to pay for the high style of living of the officers. High salaries, duty-free cars, housing, and other allowances have made officership a lucrative career for many with just a high school education. Nevertheless, there has always been some tension within the GDF between those officers who favor a more politically neutral role for the GDF and those who favor an uninhibited embrace of the PNC. So far, the latter have prevailed.

The PNC has used the GDF to aid it in securing victories at every election since 1973. At the first biennial congress of the PNC in 1974, the GDF was required to pledge its allegiance to the PNC. The chief of staff, Brigadier Clarence Price, had become too beholden to Forbes Burnham to resist this and other partisan demands. GDF soldiers are routinely subjected to political indoctrination at the Kuru-Kuru Cooperative College, and the GDF schedules marches to celebrate the congresses and other events of importance to the PNC.

The increasing subordination of the GDF to the PNC caused mutterings within the army. Some officers wondered aloud about the advisability of linking the army so closely with the fortunes of a particular political party. What encouraged this kind of questioning even more was the appearance of the WPA as a credible alternative to both the PNC and the PPP. The PNC leadership found it difficult to respond to the charges by such prominent blacks as Walter Rodney and Eusi Kwayana that the PNC was using blacks simply to retain power and to dominate both blacks and nonblacks. In a 1978 speech, Rodney raised the race issue and pointed to the type of strategy that the PNC was using. He said:

Does it have to do with race that the cost of living far outstrips the increase in wages? Does it have anything to do with race that there are no goods in the shops? Does it have anything to do with race when the original lack of democracy as exemplified in the national elections is reproduced at the level of local government elections? Does it have anything to do with race when the bauxite workers cannot elect their own union leadership? Does it have anything to do with race when, day after day, whether one is Indian or African, without the appropriate party credentials, one either gets no employment, loses one's employment, or is subject to lack of promotion? . . .

It is time that we understand that those in power are still attempting to maintain us in that mentality—maintain us captive in that mentality where we are afraid to act or we act injudiciously because we believe our racial interests are at stake. Surely we have to transcend the racial problems? Surely we have to find ways and means of ensuring that there is racial justice in this society? But it certainly will not be done by a handful of so-called Black men monopolising the power, squeezing the life out of all sections of the working class. . . . [25]

Appeals like this not only increased the WPA's multiracial following but also won sympathy for WPA within the army command.

The PNC network within the officer corps must have alerted Burnham of the potential problem he faced within the GDF. In August 1979, Burnham dismissed two of the army's most popular officers, Colonel Ulric Pilgrim, the operational force commander, and Colonel Carl Morgan, a battalion commander. Colonel David Granger, the PNC loyalist, was made commander of the GDF.[26] However, since Burnham was uncertain about whether he had contained the problem, he used this opportunity to ease out Brigadier Clarence Price from the position of chief-of-staff of the army, and instead of appointing an army officer to that position, Burnham appointed a police officer to head the army. Norman McLean, a Burnham loyalist who had at one time been the traffic chief in Guyana, was promoted to the rank of brigadier and made chief-of-staff of the army.[27] McLean's appointment affronted GDF officers and became a source of tension within the army. In 1981, the PNC regime tried to make amends by issuing a postage stamp commemorating the 16th anniversary of the GDF. The same stamp was reissued in 1985 after Burnham's death in an attempt by President Hoyte to court the loyalty of the GDF. Hoyte also promoted the two most senior officers of the GDF, a move clearly aimed at retaining the loyalty and collaboration of the GDF.

The Guyana Police Force

The Guyana Police Force contributes approximately 4,500 personnel to the country's security forces.[28] The police force has always been predominantly black and also sympathetic to the PNC, though, as in the Guyana Defense Force, political partisanship is not entirely unchallenged within the Force. Since independence, professionalism of the police force has markedly declined. As part of the structure upholding the PNC's "paramountcy," the police force has carved out a privileged position for itself. Policemen feel that they can do no wrong, or as one researcher has put it, "they have earned a public reputation for being a corrupt law unto themselves."[29] Arbitrary detention of persons with links to the opposition parties, physical abuse of arrested persons, and summary executions have all become part of regular police behavior in Guyana.[30]

The Guyana National Service

The Guyana National Service (GNS) is a para-military unit with a personnel strength of 4,500.[31] It is overwhelmingly black and very loyal to the PNC. The National Service program was an expansion of the Guyana Youth Corps program based at Tumatumari. The Youth Corps program was a voluntary effort to penetrate the interior of the country.

The program suffered from a paucity of personnel. The National Service was created in part to remedy that deficiency.

The National Service came into existence in 1974 with an original proposal that students aspiring to a higher education at the University of Guyana would be required to do one year of national service in the undeveloped interior of the country. The project was thus conceived as a way of opening up the hinterland. The National Service program was also seen as a way of imparting new skills, including military training, to Guyanese youth, of forging interracial cooperation, and of giving Guyanese youth the ideological preparation that the PNC felt was essential for the building of socialism in the country.[32]

Controversy developed very quickly over the National Service scheme as it related to young women. All of the National Service centers were to be located in the remote parts of the country. In Guyana, it is customary for unmarried young women to live at home with their parents. Those who work in urban areas away from home live with relatives or make boarding arrangements with families. This is especially true of unmarried Indian women. Indians were thus alarmed by proposals to send these young women to remote parts of the country. They saw the National Service arrangement as an attempt at forced miscegenation. This fear became heightened when it became known that 90 percent of the young women in the first group selected from the University of Guyana for national service were Indian.[33] Many of these women refused to enter the National Service program and, as a result, did not graduate from the university. Since that time, the fear of national service has kept many Indian women out of the university. Indeed, it is a very common practice among Indian families to send their daughters overseas so as to "save" them from the National Service program. Nevertheless, the National Service requirement for university students has remained unchanged.

It is widely recognized in Guyana that the National Service training centers are indoctrination centers. In fact, it was the PNC's success with the political indoctrination of the National Service that encouraged the party to embark on the political indoctrination of the army. National Service as an ideological enterprise has been extended into the elementary and secondary schools of Guyana. At the elementary school level, membership in the National Service is more or less compulsory. Students who do not participate do not receive their results from the Common Entrance Examination, which is the national high school placement examination. The students who participate are organized into the Young Brigade and are taught to march and to chant party slogans. At the high schools, students in the fourth form (junior year) are encouraged to join the National Service Cadet Corps. They perform the same functions as the Young Pioneers, except that they are taken on National Service field camps for further indoctrination.

The National Service was also developed as a counterweight to the Guyana Defense Force. Students make up only a small percentage of the National Service personnel. The vast majority of the National Service "pioneers" are full-time employees. They initially received their military training from the Guyana Defense Force. The National Service has since developed its own training cadre. Many of the National Service officers are ex-GDF officers who were enticed into the National Service by the promise of faster promotion. The director-general of the National Service, Joe Singh, was a colonel in the GDF. Also, officers who were dismissed from the GDF resurfaced in the National Service, presumably after making personal representations to the president. The National Service as a military organization is very well-trained, a fact that has registered on the officer corps of the GDF.

The People's Militia

The People's Militia is a para-military force that was established in 1976 when the Burnham regime felt that a foreign invasion was imminent. The proposal for such a militia came from Opposition Leader Cheddi Jagan who argued that the Guyana Defense Force should be replaced by an army that was more representative of the Guyanese people. Jagan's conception of the People's Militia was an organization managed by the people and having branches in every city block and every village.[34] Burnham accepted the idea of a people's militia but created one as an adjunct to the existing security forces.

The People's Militia has a strength of approximately 3,000 armed personnel.[35] It is almost entirely black. The major centers of training are located in traditional PNC strongholds. At the start of the program, Indians volunteered for training. However, there was an obvious disparity in the training given to Indian and black volunteers. In Indian areas, youths were simply taught marching drills but no skill-at-arms. In black areas, training volunteers with weapons was the norm, and photographs in the local press helped to show up the discrepancies. The result was that Indian youths became discouraged and abandoned the program. It was apparent soon after its creation that the People's Militia would simply become another component of the security forces. The People's Militia is very loyal to the PNC because of the recruitment pattern and because of continued political indoctrination. Like the National Service, the People's Militia provides the PNC with an additional counterweight to the regular army.

The National Guard Service

The National Guard Service (NGS) was established in 1980 to protect government officers and other state properties against theft or damage from subversive actions. The NGS incorporated the security personnel who were already employed at government ministries, schools, hospitals, and other government areas, but additional personnel including retired police officers were recruited The National Guard Service is approximately 2,000 members strong.[36]

The Young Socialist Movement

The Young Socialist Movement is the youth arm of the PNC. Its members are scattered all over Guyana. The YSM has succeeded in penetrating the traditional PPP areas where its recruitment drive is sustained by its ability to secure jobs for members. The YSM has a military wing with an estimated strength of about 2,000. These men have received military training provided by the GDF, the National Service, or the People's Militia. The members of this select group usually parade in military style uniforms. They do not carry arms in public. However, there are "ammunition dumps" located in various parts of the country. The YSM knows where these dumps are, and it is reasonable to assume that they would have access to them if the PNC leadership considers it necessary.

RELIGIOUS CULTS

Two major religious cults operated in Guyana under the protection of the PNC and in the service of the PNC. The one that acquired international notoriety was the People's Temple of Christ led by the Reverend Jim Jones. While the tragic denouement of Jonestown shocked all Guyanese, as it did the outside world, it was the other cult, the House of Israel, that featured more significantly in the day-to-day politics of Guyana. This was because the House of Israel became an informal part of the PNC's security apparatus and performed such services as strikebreaking, engaging in pro-government demonstrations, and carrying out acts of intimidation including murder.

The People's Temple of Christ

The domestic furor over the People's Temple arose after the mass suicide on November 18, 1978. Many Guyanese were unaware of the existence of this cult until the tragedy occurred. This was not surprising since the cult operated in the northwest of Guyana, physically isolated from the rest of Guyanese society. It was the isolation, the fact that Jonestown was governed under rules that were different from the rest of Guyana, and the possession of arms and drugs in violation of Guyanese laws that supported the charge by domestic opposition groups that Jones operated "a state within the state." The grief and embarrassment caused by the mass suicide brought forth vigorous demands from groups outside of the government for an investigation into the tragedy. Burnham, however, dismissed the tragedy as "an American affair," and no official inquiry was conducted.[37] The domestic press, which is largely government-controlled, soon dropped the matter. Much of what has been learned about the People's Temple came from the investigations of foreigners.

The People's Temple went to Guyana in 1974 with a lease to set up an agricultural community on a large tract of land near Port Kaituma in the Northwest District. Apart from his claim to be a faith healer, which he tried to demonstrate at the Sacred Heart Church in Georgetown on December 29, 1974, Reverend Jim Jones portrayed himself as a socialist. The fact that the majority of his followers were black Americans was held up as evidence of his love for the oppressed.[38]

The PNC government welcomed Jim Jones and his followers for several reasons. Jones's plan for an agricultural commune fitted with the government's plan to open up Guyana's hinterland, and Jones had brought in a large sum of money for investment in the country.[39] The project had even greater significance because the acreage leased to the People's Temple was located in the region claimed by Venezuela to be part of its territory (see Chapter 6). By setting up an agricultural community of Americans in the disputed area, Jones would be helping the Guyana government settle this area without provoking the kind of response from Venezuela that would likely have come if the settlers were Guyana nationals. Finally, Jim Jones went to Guyana with an impressive list of references. He even claimed President Jimmy Carter and the First Lady to be among his well-wishers. In this regard, Jones was able to exploit a lingering fear of the Burnham government about possible U.S. intervention in Guyana over the nationalization of the bauxite companies. Jones assured the Burnham government that he would use his influence with the White House to ensure nonintervention in Guyana.[40]

Once in Guyana, the People's Temple courted the country's rulers in a variety of ways. Jim Jones spoke of Guyana as a model of socialism and pledged the Temple's loyalty to the PNC.[41] Linda Amos, who was in charge of the Temple's office in Georgetown, became a member of the Women's Revolutionary Socialist Movement, the women's auxiliary of the PNC, headed by Burnham's wife, Viola. The People's Temple members took part in marches in behalf of the PNC. Temple members may also have voted in the controversial July 1978 referendum.[42]

The Temple also arranged sexual affairs with political and governmental officials to gain influence with them. These duties were assigned to Paula Adams, whom James Reston described as Jones's "professional prostitute."[43] One of her clients was Lawrence Mann, then Guyana's ambassador to the United States.[44] Linda Amos "developed a strategic relationship with the Chief Justice of Guyana, Harold Bollers."[45] The Temple's leaders no doubt saw this liaison as potentially useful in protecting them in legal actions brought by relatives of cult members or by excult members. The Temple entertained political notables in great style at their Georgetown office at Lamaha Gardens. As one guest described it, "You could have drowned yourself in liquor, all types of liquor. You name it, it was there."[46] These influence campaigns plus the success of the commune as an agricultural entity assured the Temple of noninterference by officials of the Guyana government.

The People's Temple also used sex to facilitate the smuggling of guns into Guyana. Guns were generally smuggled in false-bottomed crates and were cleared through customs by attractive Temple women who flirted with the customs officials to ensure that the containers for Jonestown were not carefully examined. The following memorandum by Linda Amos indicates that attempts were made to get to know the customs inspectors before sensitive shipments were to be cleared: "Two men from customs came and danced with Karen [Layton] and me (they dance very close) and were obnoxious. But we were friendly to them, and one of them was there when the stuff came through customs."[47] Presumably, drugs were also smuggled in this way.

As is now quite well-known, the Jonestown commune ended in a mass suicide in which 914 people died. A cult that operated outside of the mainstream of Guyanese life became a source of grief and embarrassment to all Guyanese. Walter Rodney was attempting to capture more than just the impact of Jonestown when he said, "Wherever we go, 'we shame'. "[48] The fact that the PNC government refused to conduct an investigation into a tragedy of this magnitude was yet additional evidence of the divorcement, on the part of the PNC, of the question of rulership and the question of public accountability. It was also evidence of the absence from the PNC of any fear of being penalized at the polls for this tragedy or for any other.

The House of Israel

The House of Israel was a religious cult that was protected by the PNC and which provided a thug force for the party. In fact, the colors of the uniforms of cult members were the colors of the PNC: black, red, and green. The House of Israel was headed by "Rabbi" Edward Washington, a black-American fugitive who is wanted by the FBI for an assortment of crimes including blackmail, larceny, and income tax evasion. Washington, whose real name is David Hill, fled to Guyana while he was on bail. He presented himself to the PNC leadership as a victim of racist American politics. As Washington himself put it, "I came to Guyana in 1972. I had found that there is no justice in my own country for people of my colour. This is why many blacks are fleeing the U.S. and going to live in Third World countries."[49]

Despite its name, the House of Israel was not directly related to either the state of Israel or to Jewish religious practices. Instead it was a black supremacist cult which claimed that blacks were the original Hebrews and that those who today call themselves Jews are, in fact, Edomites and are in Israel illegally.[50] The cult leadership was preparing its followers for a racial Armageddon. The House of Israel had a daily radio program which the "Rabbi" used to preach a racial religious message. The cult boasted a membership of about 8,000, which included other black-American fugitives. The cult served as a private army for the PNC. According to the WPA, "it is the PNC that armed the House of Israel and gave them military training. . . . The PNC not only supplied the House of Israel with G3s and other arms, but with military uniforms."[51]

The House of Israel acquired a reputation for ruthlessness after one of its members committed a public murder in July 1979. On July 14, Bilal Ato, a cult member, stabbed and killed an English Jesuit priest in full public view. Fr. Bernard Darke, who was the photographer for the *Catholic Standard*, was photographing a public demonstration outside of a magistrate's court a few hundred yards from the Brickdam Police Station when he was attacked and killed by the cult member.[52] A few days later, Walter Rodney accused the government of being behind the murder. Rodney said:

The WPA has publicly accused the PNC as a party and as the government of this country, of complicity in that murder, and we have said that in any decent and civilized country, investigations would have proceeded to find out who were the real authors and instigators of the murder of Father Darke. (Someone shouts, "Rabbi.") More than just the Rabbi. We must not be confused into thinking that the Rabbi is an independent entity! The Rabbi is not independent. The Rabbi himself is a stooge of other forces. We must identify his masters— his paymasters. We must not be afraid to say openly that the People's National Congress has been officially involved in thuggery. Eventually it had to lead to murder as it did on July the fourteenth.[53]

Although the entire incident was photographed by other journalists, it took the government three years to bring the case to trial. The assassin, Bilal Ato, was defended by a lawyer who had acted as the state prosecutor in other cases. Ato's charge was reduced to manslaughter, and he received an eight-year sentence.[54] However, it is widely believed that Ato is receiving special consideration as he serves out this sentence.

The House of Israel performed an assortment of other sordid services for the PNC. They were employed in strike-breaking activities and were frequently used to disrupt the public meetings of groups opposed to the ruling party. On those occasions, they appeared in the company of the police, and sometimes wore police uniforms. Eusi Kwayana described one such incident that occurred on August 22, 1979, just as the WPA leaders were about to address a public meeting.

Suddenly a squad of uniformed policemen, including Rabbi Washington's men dressed in police uniform and carrying no regulation numbers, attacked the meeting which they claimed was illegal. It was a total assault with batons on the crowd of peaceful citizens by a crowd of well-armed policemen of the Tactical Service Unit (Riot Squad). Soon the crowd burst and scattered from the meeting point at Delph Street and Campbell Avenue and dashed for Middleton Street and then across it to Kitty. Scores of people were beaten by the police. They were on fire with a venom not noticed before. This was due to the House of Israel. Brother Moses Bhagwan who took refuge with some livestock in a nearby yard was dragged out and beaten, ending with a broken arm. After that he was arrested and charged.[55]

Forbes Burnham, referring to this incident, commented on Walter Rodney's prowess as an athlete and promised to send Rodney to the Olympics![56]

In July 1986, Rabbi Washington and key associates were arrested and charged with a 1977 murder of the husband of a cult member. Washington pleaded guilty to the lesser charge of manslaughter and was sentenced to 15 years in prison.[57] The fact that it took the government nine years to bring Washington to trial was clear evidence that he enjoyed the protection of the regime. The Rabbi became a casualty of President Hoyte's efforts to win support within the population by giving his authoritarian regime a more humane outlook. Nevertheless, the *Catholic Standard* used the occasion to again draw the link between the House of Israel and the PNC. Its November 6, 1986, editorial read, "That the 'Rabbi' and his cult could not have functioned without official patronage is amply borne out by their complete abandonment now that the patronage has been withdrawn. The 'Rabbi' himself told us that in the killing of Fr. Darke, his men acted on the instructions of top members of the party."[58]

A REIGN OF TERROR

Since 1980, Indian communities in Guyana have been subjected to some of the most savage crimes by organized gangs of blacks. The gangs are commonly known in Guyana as the "kick-down-the-door gangs," because of their peculiar mode of operation. The gangs are fully armed and display a commando style of operation. They would kick down the doors of homes, rob the family, inflict physical violence on family members, including raping women and young girls, and in some cases, even killing members of the family.[59]

The response of the police has been severely criticized within Guyana. The police consistently arrive at the homes hours after the crimes have been committed, even in those cases when the police were notified of a crime in progress. The pattern of police response over the years seems to have been reassuring to the gangs that have increased in number and in the scope of their crimes; some of which occur even in the daytime. So great is the fear in Indian communities that housewives in rural areas spend much of their day congregating by the public roads, fearful of being victims of violence in the relative isolation of their homes. In July 1985, Eusi Kwayana and Rupert Roopnarain of the WPA led a "Freedom Walk" across the country. In a commentary on the "Freedom Walk," the *Catholic Standard* noted that "A disturbing feature of the Walkers was the sight of Indo-Guyanese women in the Corentyne out in the road during the middle of the day, afraid to be in their homes for fear of rape and robbery."[60]

There are several aspects of this violence that suggest PNC sponsorship or acquiescence. The first is that the violence, which the police seemed incapable of handling, suddenly abated in mid–1986. The abatement coincided with the talks between the Guyana government and the United States government regarding the resumption of U.S. aid to Guyana.[61] The U.S. State Department, in its annual human rights reports, has been critical of the Guyana government's human rights record. It is reasonable to assume that the State Department used the talks with the representatives of the Guyana government to express U.S. concern about the PNC's human rights record. Nevertheless, the suddenness with which the "kick-down-the-door" violence abated suggests that the PNC government has always had leverage over the gangs.

The second noteworthy aspect of the violence concerns the sophistication of the weapons used. The gang members wear military boots and are armed with automatic weapons. However, Guyana has strict gun control laws, and the security forces enjoy a monopoly of access to arms. This raises the troubling question about how the gangs are being armed. One commentator refers to gang members as "policemen by day and bandits by night."[62] Indeed, it cannot be ruled out that some of the gang members might be military and police personnel in civilian clothes. Rabbi Washington confessed that cult members were involved in burglaries.[63]

A third observation about this violence is that, except for the scale and the brutality in the 1980s, it bears a strong resemblance to a tactic used by the PNC in 1979 when it feared that blacks were deserting the party for the WPA. At public meetings of the opposition parties, but particularly at WPA public meetings, bands of blacks, generally believed to be members of the House of Israel, were employed by the PNC to cause disruptions by attacking Indians who were present. Although police officers were usually present at these meetings, the assailants were not arrested, suggesting that these acts of violence had official sanction.[64] The purpose of these racially selective attacks seemed to be to prevent blacks and Indians from uniting against the ruling party. The hope no doubt was that Indians would develop resentment toward blacks, while blacks, fearing Indian retaliation, would seek the protection of the PNC. The tactic did not succeed but it persisted. The gang violence against Indian communities since 1980 seems to be a national application of the tactic to keep ethnic antagonism alive. It has certainly succeeded in creating a heightened sense of ethnic xenophobia among Indians in rural areas.

The crimes against the Indians in Guyana can also be viewed as a perverse form of patronage. The thugs who perpetrate these crimes appear to be the same ones who avail themselves to the ruling party to be used as recycled voters in national elections and to intimidate opposition parties, that is, they commit crimes for the PNC and expect the PNC government to look the other way when they commit crimes for their own survival. The crimes are committed against Indians, who have generally not been supporters of the PNC, and in times of severe food shortages when the government cannot satisfy the needs of its supporters, it may simply be permitting some of them to help themselves.

THE MEDIA

The government controls the media in Guyana. The media, like the security forces, are used to peddle government and party propaganda and to criticize opponents of the ruling party. An opposition press does exist, but the government uses the courts and its control over the importation of newsprint to smother competing sources of information.

There is one radio station in Guyana and it is government-owned. It is called the Guyana Broadcasting Station. Until 1975, it had a rival of sorts in the privately-owned station, Radio Demerara, which was also the older radio station. However, the government bought Radio Demerara and combined its operations with the Guyana Broadcasting Station. The radio station functions almost entirely in the interest of the PNC, Guyana's "paramount" institution. Even "Action Line," an evening call-in program, is rigged to cast the governing party in a favorable light while criticizing opposition groups.

The government also owns the only daily newspaper, the *Guyana*

Chronicle. It acquired this paper in 1974 when it bought the *Guyana Graphic* from Lord Thompson and renamed it. As the British Parliamentary Human Rights Group observed, the paper reads "like an election address for the PNC."[65] The subservience of the paper to the ruling party can be recognized in a memorandum issued by the editor of the paper to the staff on January 16, 1980. The memorandum states that "Only the Comrade Prime Minister, the Deputy Prime Minister and the Minister of State for Information will be responsible for the issuing of political directions and this will be done to the General Manager and Editor only."[66] In addition to the *Guyana Chronicle*, the PNC publishes a separate party newspaper called the *New Nation*. The *New Nation* focuses almost entirely on the activities of the "Comrade Leader." Both of these papers are printed on high quality newsprint.

The principal alternative sources of published information up until 1986 were the two weeklies, the *Mirror*, published by the PPP, and the *Catholic Standard*, published by the Catholic body in Guyana. The government controls these papers indirectly through its control over the importation of newsprint into the country. Scarce foreign exchange is the government's reason for controlling newsprint importation. However, only the non-PNC papers are adversely affected. The *Guyana Chronicle* and the *New Nation* are amply supplied. The government has prevented the *Mirror* and the *Catholic Standard* from accepting donations of newsprint from overseas. In 1979, the Caribbean Press and Broadcasting Association offered to donate five tons of newsprint to the *Mirror*, but the government prevented the *Mirror* from accepting the newsprint. Offers of newsprint donations to the *Catholic Standard* by the papal nuncio in Trinidad, and by the Canadian Council of Churches have been refused by the government without explanation.[67] All of this clearly suggests that the sole motivation behind the restrictions on newsprint is political.

The Soviet Union was apparently concerned about the PPP's inability to publish. In 1985 it capitalized on the conciliatory atmosphere attending the "constructive dialogue" that the PNC had initiated with the PPP and made a gift of newsprint to both the PNC and the PPP. On this occasion, the PPP was allowed to accept the gift. Although the *Catholic Standard* continues to receive offers of newsprint from church groups and others overseas, the government has prevented acceptance.[68]

Since the *Mirror* is the organ of the PPP and since the *Guyana Chronicle* and the *New Nation* are mouthpieces of the PNC, the *Catholic Standard* was, until 1986, the only independent newspaper in the country. Governmental efforts to suppress it go far beyond denying it newsprint. The editors of the *Catholic Standard* have been subjected to death threats. This was the case with Fr. Wong, particularly after the 1973 election, and continues to be the case with Fr. Andrew Morrison, his successor.

In July 1979, Fr. Bernard Darke, the priest who was then the photographer for the *Catholic Standard*, was stabbed to death while photographing a demonstration. The assistant editor of the paper, Michael James, was badly beaten at the same location.[69]

The government also uses libel suits in an effort to pressure the *Catholic Standard*. In 1984, there were four such suits against the paper.[70] They were brought against the paper by PNC officials. Since the cases are tried in courts controlled by the government, the paper can expect to pay large punitive fines. Fortunately for the paper, past fines have been paid by donations. The result is that the paper survives and continues to be a thorn in the side of the government.

Various other news sheets have been circulated by opposition parties. The *Vanguard* was a news sheet put out by the Vanguard for Liberation and Democracy. Both the party and the paper have ceased to exist. The WPA publishes two weekly news sheets, the *Dayclean* and the *Open Word*.

In 1986, the PNC government gave permission for the launching of a privately-owned newspaper. The initiators of this enterprise were two lawyers, David De Caires and Miles Fitzpatrick. The newspaper, called the *Stabroek News*, is published weekly. It is printed on the presses of the *Express* of Trinidad-and-Tobago and transported to Guyana. The foreign exchange required for the operation of this newspaper is raised overseas. In fact, the paper began with a start-up grant of U.S. $110,000, provided by the National Endowment for Democracy, an American foundation.[71] Because the Guyana government has used its control over foreign exchange allocation to create difficulties for local publishers, the survival of the *Stabroek News* will depend on the continued ability of its promoters to cultivate foreign donors.

TRADE UNIONS

Guyana's socialist constitution recognizes the right to form trade unions for the purpose of collective bargaining. Trade unions have always played a major role in Guyana and, in fact, antedate mass-based political parties in Guyana. Trade unions have also been actively involved in the politics of the country and it is very common to find political leaders also heading trade unions. For example, Cheddi Jagan, the leader of the PPP, is the honorary president of the Guyana Agricultural Workers' Union; and President Forbes Burnham, until his death in August 1985, was the president of the Guyana Labor Union.

The umbrella organization for organized labor in Guyana is the Trades Union Congress (TUC). Since the 1960s, the TUC has been dominated by PNC-affiliated unions. Until 1976, the Manpower Citizens' Association, which was the recognized sugar union, played a pivotal role in ensuring PNC control over the TUC. The MPCA represented the largest number of workers and therefore had the largest number of delegates to the annual conference that elected the executive. In 1976, when the PNC government permitted a poll in the sugar industry to determine the union preference of the sugar workers, it realized that the MPCA would be replaced by the PPP-affiliated union, GAWU. In anticipation of GAWU's entry into the TUC, the executive of the TUC reworked the formula for the selection of delegates in a manner that would diminish the impact of GAWU's strength. The result was an inequitable arrangement in which GAWU with a membership of over 15,000 has 1 delegate for every 442 members, while the Guyana Cooperative Mortgage Finance Bank Staff Association has 1 delegate for every 13 members. By this means, the PNC was able to retain control over the TUC until October 1984.[72] Evidence of PNC control lay in the fact that between 1982 and 1984, the minister of labor, Kenneth Denny, the principal governmental official that the TUC had to deal with, was the organizing secretary of the TUC, and the minister of finance, Salim Salahuddin, was a member of the TUC executive.[73]

In March 1984, the PNC government moved to consolidate its control over organized labor. By the Labour Amendment Act of March 1984, the government deprived individual unions of the right to negotiate agreements for their members and made the TUC the sole bargaining agent for all public sector employees.[74] Since 51 percent of the Guyanese work force are employed in the public sector, and since the PNC controlled the TUC, the Labour Amendment Act spelled the emasculation of organized labor. To the great consternation of the PNC, however, there was a revolt at the TUC elections in October 1984, and the PNC candidates for the TUC executive were defeated by candidates who claimed to be more independent minded.[75] The immediate cause of the revolt within the TUC was the Labour Amendment Act. However, the revolt was also evidence that even the pro-PNC union leaders could no longer ignore the strong dissatisfaction of their rank-and-file members with the deteriorating economic conditions and with the collaborative role that the TUC was playing vis-à-vis the PNC government.

Active resistance to PNC control of the TUC probably began with the entry of the pro-PPP sugar union, GAWU, into the TUC in 1976. GAWU had established a reputation as Guyana's most militant trade union. In 1976, there were 284 strikes in the country of which 234 were in the sugar industry. In 1983, the year before the critical TUC election, there were 731 strikes in the country and 704 of these were in the sugar industry.[76] GAWU became the spearhead of resistance to PNC control of the TUC. It should be pointed out that at the time of GAWU's entry into the TUC, there were three other unions within the organization that were opposed to PNC control. These were the National Association of Agricultural, Clerical, and Industrial Employees (NAACIE), a small but very visible pro-PPP union in the sugar industry; the University of Guyana Staff Association (USGA), which is WPA-affiliated; and the Clerical and Commercial Workers' Union (CCWU), an urban union of store clerks, whose president, Gordon Todd, is opposed to the control of any union by a political party.[77]

Shortly after it entered the TUC, GAWU established an alliance with the three non-PNC unions. The remaining 19 unions within the TUC were affiliated to the PNC. However, PNC control was being challenged in the larger bauxite union, the Guyana Mine Workers' Union (GMWU). With a membership of about 6,000, the GMWU was the largest industrial union under PNC control. In 1976, a dissident faction within the GMWU attempted to wrest control of the union from the PNC-affiliated executive. Through a rigged election, the PNC loyalists were able to retain control. However, PNC control over the GMWU executive did not prevent a wage strike, called by the workers themselves, in the bauxite industry in December 1976. The government threatened the workers with dismissal, but what really enraged the mining community was the arrest and teargassing, while in police custody, of 42 of the strike leaders.[78] Dissatisfaction with the PNC began to spread in the mining community and the effort to take the union out of PNC control intensified. At the TUC-sponsored rally at the National Park on May Day, the guest speaker, Forbes Burnham, was heckled and booed.[79] This was the first time, since assuming office, that this had happened to Burnham at a gathering of the faithful.

In August 1979, the bauxite workers were again on strike for wages. The strike, which started out at the mining operations at Kwakwani, became a general strike in the industry and was eventually sanctioned by the GMWU executive. Solidarity strikes were also called by the GAWU, NAACIE, and the CCWU.[80] Burnham declared the strikes to be political and warned that "this government will not sit idly by and permit reactionary zealots to ruin the economy and jeopardize the well-being of the workers and the nation."[81] The strike was forcefully repressed with the aid of the police and the House of Israel. In one instance, according to Kwayana, "workers were beaten up in broad daylight by a band of official thugs led by Hamilton Green, now Vice President. House of Israel thugs appeared in many guises beating up Indo-Guyanese and Afro-Guyanese."[82] Kwayana also noted that "Gordon Todd [president of the CCWU] was arrested for appearing with his members in public and taken off to a military outpost and held incommunicado for several hours until the TUC General Secretary J. H. Pollydore intervened with the Prime Minister Burnham, who it would seem, had not left these details to mere assistants."[83]

By 1982, conditions of life in Guyana had become so difficult that even the pro-PNC unions in the TUC felt that something had to be done. At their November meeting, the TUC delegates decided to protest against the government's proposed increase in electricity rates, as well as the harsh economic conditions facing Guyanese workers. A TUC-sponsored protest march was held in Georgetown on December 15. This was the first time, since the PNC took office, that the TUC had organized a protest against the government.[84]

Trade union pressure against the government continued in 1983 with strikes in the bauxite and sugar industries. The previous year, the pro-PNC executive of the Guyana Mine Workers' Union, as well as that of the smaller Guyana Bauxite Supervisors' Association (GBSA), was replaced by more independently-minded leadership. On May 19, 1983, under their new leadership, the bauxite workers staged a protest march against the shortages of food and drugs and announced that they would strike for one day a week until the situation was improved. The PNC government responded by cutting their five-day work week to a three-day work week. On June 2, bauxite workers went on a six-week strike in order to restore their normal five-day work week. They were supported by sugar workers who went on strike once a week. "Unity committees" were set up to coordinate the distribution of limited food supplies between the strikers in the two industries. The strike ended when the government agreed to restore the five-day work week and the bauxite workers agreed to give up their one-day-a-week strike. Then, in an act described by TUC General Secretary Joseph Pollydore as "vengeful discrimination," the government fired 1,721 bauxite workers, or approximately 29 percent of the work force.[85] It was not surprising, therefore, that at the end of the strike, both bauxite unions—the GMWU and the GBSA—joined GAWU, NAACIE, CCWU, and UGSA to form a six-union non-PNC bloc within the TUC.[86]

The following year, the six-union bloc was joined by the second largest union in Guyana, the Public Service Union (PSU). The PSU was the former Civil Service Association (CSA) that had played a major role in the 1963 strike against the PPP government. There were several reasons why the PSU joined the "opposition" unions in the TUC. The government had been engaged in a massive retrenchment of public sector employees since 1978 when it signed an agreement with the International Monetary Fund (IMF). Between 1980 and 1983, the number of employees in the public sector shrunk by approximately 24,000.[87] Many of the people who lost their jobs were PSU members. Secondly, the astronomical increase in the cost of living had had a devastating impact on PSU members, most of whom are urban dwellers. Between 1978 and 1983, the consumer price index increased by approximately 250 percent.[88] Thirdly, the PSU was opposed to the Labour Amendment Act that would deprive it of the bargaining power it traditionally enjoyed.[89]

In the 1984 TUC elections, the president of the PSU, George Daniels, became the "opposition" candidate for the office of president of the TUC, which he won. He defeated the PNC-supported candidate, Jean Persico of the Guyana Teachers' Association. The PNC minister, Kenneth Denny, was defeated by Lincoln Lewis of the Guyana Mine Workers' Union for the position of organizing secretary of the TUC. It should be pointed out that the seven non-PNC unions did not have the delegate strength to win these positions by themselves. They were supported by 26 delegates from the PNC-affiliated unions, a clear indication of a dissatisfaction with the status quo even among PNC-affiliated unions.[90]

The new TUC leadership has the potential to cause tremendous problems for the government, particularly with its legal right to bargain for all public sector employees. However, the government has resorted to the tactic of preempting negotiations with the TUC by unilaterally determining wage increases for public sector employees.[91] It is also seeking to regain control of the TUC.

CHURCH-STATE RELATIONS

Guyana's socialist constitution guarantees the freedom of religion. Fifty-seven percent of the Guyanese population are Christians, while Hindus and Muslims account for 33 percent and 9 percent, respectively.[92] The practice of obeah, a form of African witchcraft, was legalized in 1970 by the PNC regime. There is no state religion, although the Anglican Church enjoyed that status prior to independence.

Almost all of the Hindus and Muslims are Indians and have traditionally identified with the PPP. However, the PNC has succeeded in splitting the leadership of the Hindu and Muslim organizations so that in each case, there is a pro-PNC faction and a pro-PPP faction. Thus, the leadership of the Sanatan Dharma Maha Sabha and the Pandits Council are pro-PNC, while the Hindu Dharmic Sabha is pro-PPP. In the case of Muslim organizations, the United Sad'r Islamic Anjuman and the Islamic Missionary Guild are pro-PNC, while the Central Islamic Organization of Guyana is pro-PPP. The PNC has had a much more difficult time with the Christian churches, and it is this aspect of church-state relations that has been the most tense and the most troublesome for the regime.

The umbrella organization of the Christian churches is the Guyana Council of Churches (GCC). Within this organization, leadership has, until recently, been provided by the Roman Catholic and the Anglican clergy. Although the GCC has emerged as one of the most vocal critics of the PNC regime, this has been a relatively recent development.

Prior to the 1968 election, the Roman Catholic Church in Guyana was very strongly identified with the United Force. It was common knowledge that Catholic priests used their pulpits to canvass for the United Force. After the 1968 election, Peter D'Aguiar resigned as party leader and the party began to languish. In any case, the D'Aguiar resignation was widely interpreted as reflective of a realization on the part of the UF leadership that the party could never achieve political power in Guyana. At about this time, the Catholic Church began to cast off its conservatism and to publicly demonstrate its concern about social, economic, and political conditions in the country and about the impact these were having on Christians and on the Guyanese population generally. Editorials and other articles in the *Catholic Standard* began to reflect this change in the orientation of the Catholic Church.

The PNC regime would like to contain the influence of the Catholic Church and has attempted, without success, to snuff out the *Catholic Standard*. The regime has been more successful in limiting the number of Catholic priests in Guyana. Many of the Jesuit priests are foreign-born, and the regime has used this to force many of them to leave the country. The regime has also restricted the access of priests to the Amerindians in the interior of the country.[93] All of these measures, however, have increased the sympathy of the Guyanese toward the Catholic Church.

The other Christian denominations were much slower in voicing their opposition to the abuses of the regime. In the churches located in urban areas, support of the PNC regime was strong because of the predominantly black composition of the congregations. However, in the latter part of the 1970s, these churches began to line up against the regime as economic hardships mounted and as the regime's abuses increased. The first to do so was the Anglican Church. The Anglican and the Catholic churches unsuccessfully opposed the regime's decision in 1976 to take over the denominational schools, most of which were owned by the Catholic and the Anglican churches.[94]

Thereafter, the Guyana Council of Churches became more vocal in its criticisms of governmental abuses. It opposed the government's purpose in holding the 1978 referendum and criticized the conduct of the referendum. It accused the government of fraud in the 1980 and the 1985 elections. Because of the GCC's credibility overseas, the regime is very threatened by the statements and activities of this organization. The PNC's response has taken the form of harassment of church leaders. On March 12, 1985, the PNC used cult members of the House of Israel to occupy the church-owned Diocesan Youth Centre and thereby prevented the holding of the annual meeting of the Guyana Council of Churches.[95] On December 17, 1985, the homes of several church leaders were searched by the police for arms. Those affected by the search were Catholic Bishop Benedict Singh, Anglican Bishop Randolph George, Rev. George Richmond, Chairman of the GCC and head of the Moravian

Church, and Rev. Oswald Best, head of the Presbyterian Church.[96] The persecution of church leaders, most of whom are black, has enhanced the stature of these men and has drawn increased international attention to the excesses of the PNC regime.

THE EDUCATIONAL SYSTEM

The educational system in Guyana is entirely under government control. Control is centralized in the Ministry of Education. In 1976, the PNC regime committed itself to providing free education from kindergarten to university. However, the quality of that education has deteriorated enormously over the past decade.[97] One indicator of this is the performance of Guyana's high school students in the General Certificate of Education, a standardized examination set by the University of London, which determines whether the students will graduate from high school. Guyana's students have been performing so badly that the government has put restrictions on the disclosure of examination statistics.

There are several reasons for the deterioration of the educational system. The government appears to be unable to fund this program of free education. It does not keep the school buildings in good repair, and there are shortages of textbooks, exercise books, and other instructional materials. Further, the generally poor performance of the economy has fed back into the educational system with disastrous results. In the 1980s, two dominant public issues have been the shortage of food and the outbreak of diseases such as beriberi and scurvy. Children of school age are simply not properly fed. The fainting of students at both elementary and high schools is a common occurrence. The problems of school children are further compounded by inadequate transportation. The government has failed to keep the state-owned bus system in good working order. For a while, the government employed the "tandem system" to take students to school. The system involved using one bus in good working order to pull another bus whose engine had been taken out. Students rode in both buses, at a risk to themselves and in violation of Guyana's road safety laws. The transportation problem was eased somewhat in 1984 when the Cuban government presented the Guyana government with a fleet of buses.

Despite these problems, the regime has continued to politicize the educational system. In what seems to be an attempt to imitate the Cubans and the Soviets, the PNC regime has been trying to develop in the students a commitment to socialism. This is done through the curriculum and also through the National Service.[98] The National Service units at the elementary and secondary schools serve as vehicles to indoctrinate students. The goal is to get students to grow to accept the paramountcy of the PNC over all national institutions. Students at elementary and secondary schools are required to attend political rallies, to line the roads for official visitors, and to engage in North Korean-style mass games.

The regime also conducts periodic witch hunts in the teaching profession. Teachers, who are critical of the government's policies or are suspected of being sympathetic to opposition parties, may be arbitrarily dismissed or transferred in a manner that would inflict some degree of hardship on the teachers. Tremendous insecurity exists in the teaching profession in Guyana, with obvious ill effects on the quality of instruction.

The result of all of this has been a marked deterioration in the quality of the educational system in Guyana. Truancy and illiteracy have increased, and students perform poorly in the traditional examinations that both elementary and secondary school students are required to take.

The University of Guyana is similarly affected. The university offers undergraduate degrees in the arts and sciences and a limited number of master's degrees. The university has suffered from an exodus of qualified staff and from direct political interference by the PNC. The ruling party keeps many of the faculty and students under surveillance.

On the other hand, the PNC maintains several ideological establishments that are lavished with scarce resources. The Kuru-Kuru Cooperative College was established to train managers for cooperative enterprises. It has also become an indoctrination center where civil servants as well as military personnel are sent for short courses. The party also runs the Cuffy Ideological Institute for the training of party activists. Advancement in certain sectors of the economy is contingent on "a successful completion of theoretical and practical courses at Kuru-Kuru and Cuffy Ideological Institute."[99] In 1984, the government began the construction of the President's College. This is to be Guyana's "School of Excellence," where students will be trained to inculcate "the cooperative ethic and an ideological commitment to socialism."[100] Teachers for the President's College will receive their training in Cuba.

NOTES

1. *The Laws of Guyana: The Constitution*, pp. 31–34.
2. *Ibid.*, pp. 35–36.
3. *Ibid.*, pp. 48–54.
4. Nascimento and Burrowes, eds., *A Destiny to Mould*, p. 112.
5. *The Laws of Guyana: The Constitution*, pp. 44–48.
6. *Ibid,*. pp. 111–117.
7. *Ibid.*, pp. 57–61.
8. Burnham, *Declaration of Sophia*, p. 11.
9. *Constitution, People's National Congress of Guyana, approved by the Special Congress of PNC held at Sophia on December 14th–15th, 1974*, p. 44. See also Eusi

Kwayana, "Guyana—The Second Republic," *Caribbean Contact* (November 1981), p. 17.

10. Guyana Human Rights Association, *Human Rights Report Jan. 1980 - June 1981*, p. 8.

11. Rickey Singh, "Guyana—where absolute power belongs to President Forbes Burnham," *Caribbean Contact* (November 1980), p. 7.

12. Mahu Mahida, "Power galore for Guyana's Ruling party," *Caribbean Contact* (January 1977), p. 17.

13. *Constitution of the Co-operative Republic of Guyana* (Ruimveldt: Guyana National Lithographic Co. Ltd., 1980), p. 21.

14. *Ibid.*, p. 23.

15. *Ibid.*, p. 30.

16. *Ibid.*, pp. 34–36.

17. *Ibid.*, pp. 30–34.

18. *Ibid.*, p. 37.

19. *Ibid.*, pp. 37–38.

20. *Ibid.*, pp. 86–87.

21. *Ibid.*, pp. 92–93.

22. *Ibid.*, pp. 40–42.

23. "The Military Balance 1983–84," *Air Force Magazine* (December 1983), p. 125.

24. The author of this book served as an officer in the Guyana Defense Force from September 1973 to October 1974.

25. Walter Rodney, *In Defence of Arnold Rampersand* (Georgetown: Working People's Alliance, 1982), pp. 8–9.

26. "Guyana: Trial of the 'Referendum Five'," p. 96.

27. Singh, "The Guyanese people have had enough of their prime minister's 'eye pass'," p. 11.

28. "Power struggle looks likely after Forbes Burnham's death," *Latin American Weekly Report* (August 16, 1985), p. 1.

29. George K. Danns, "The Role of the Military in the National Security of Guyana," in Alma H. Young and Dion E. Phillips, eds., *Militarization in the Non-Hispanic Caribbean* (Boulder: Lynne Rienner Publishers, Inc., 1986), p. 129.

30. *Ibid.*, pp. 128–129; See also, *Country Reports on Human Rights Practices: Report Submitted to the Committee on Foreign Relations, U.S. Senate and Committee on Foreign Affairs, U.S. House of Representatives by the Department of State* (Washington, D.C.: U.S. Government Printing Office, 1981), p. 451; Guyana Human Rights Association, *Guyana Human Rights Report 1985* (Georgetown: Guyana Human Rights Association, 1985), pp. 14–16.

31. "Power struggle looks likely . . . ," p. 1.

32. "National Service and Socialism," *Caribbean Contact* (August 1976), p. 6.

33. Janet Jagan, *An Examination of National Service* (Georgetown: New Guyana Company Ltd., 1977), p. 10. See also, "No National Service, so no degrees," *Caribbean Contact* (January 1977), p. 15; and "Two Views of Guyana's National Service," *Caribbean Contact* (February 1978), pp. 10–11.

34. "For a National Front Government," Central Committee Document, People's Progressive Party, August 1977, p. 30.

35. "Power struggle looks likely . . . ," p. 1.

36. Danns, "The Role of the Military . . . ," pp. 127–128.

37. "Forgetting the Past," *Catholic Standard*, November 16, 1986, p. 2.

38. Rickey Singh, "Temple Massacre Could Have Been Stopped!" *Caribbean Contact* (December 1978), pp. 1–8; see also, "How the Temple came to Guyana," *Chronicle Special*, December 6, 1978, pp. 2–3, 31.

39. Estimates of the initial investment vary from a quarter of a million dollars to four million dollars. See Singh, "Temple Massacre . . . ," p. 6; and James Reston, Jr., *Our Father Who Art In Hell* (New York: Times Books, 1981), p. 148.

40. Reston, *Our Father Who Art In Hell*, pp. 158–160; George Klineman, Sherman Butler, and David Conn, *The Cult That Died* (New York: G. P. Putnam's Sons, 1980), p. 286.

41. Reston, *Our Father Who Art In Hell*, p. 148.

42. Shiva Naipaul, *Journey To Nowhere: A New World Tragedy* (New York: Simon and Schuster, 1981), pp. 48, 66.

43. Reston, *Our Father Who Art In Hell*, p. 162.

44. Klineman, et al., *The Cult That Died*, pp. 285, 310.

45. Reston, *Our Father Who Art In Hell*, p. 165.

46. Ibid., p. 287.

47. Klineman, et al., *The Cult That Died*, p. 296.

48. Rodney, *The Struggle Goes On!*, p. 9.

49. Steve Narine, "House of Israel—'no People's Temple'," *Chronicle Special*, December 6, 1978, p. 31.

50. "Fears over 'House of Israel'," *Caribbean Contact* (January 1976), p. 11; "Will FBI get fugitives hiding in Guyana?" *Caribbean Contact* (February 1979), pp. 17–18; "Rabbi Washington, American Fugitive," *The West Indian Graphic* (August 1986), p. 4.

51. "Rabbi: No Firearm Charges?" *Open Word*, September 15, 1986, p. 3.

52. Kwayana, *Walter Rodney*, pp. 24–25.

53. Rodney, *The Struggle Goes On!*, pp. 1–2.

54. *Country Reports on Human Rights Practices for 1982: Report Submitted to the Committee on Foreign Relations, U.S. Senate and Committee on Foreign Affairs, U.S. House of Representatives by the Department of State* (Washington, D.C.: U.S. Government Printing Office, 1983), p. 535.

55. Kwayana, *Walter Rodney*, p. 16.

56. *Ibid.*

57. "Rabbi Arrested, Charged With Murder," *Expo Caribbean Awake* (September 1986), pp. 1–3; Hugh Hamilton, "Guyana: The Rabbi's Great Fall: Finally, He's Jailed for 15 Years," *The West Indian Graphic* (November 1986), p.2; "Rabbi Let Off On Murder Charge," *Catholic Standard*, November 9, 1986, p. 4.

58. "Real Break With Past?" *Catholic Standard*, November 9, 1986, p. 2.

59. Guyana Human Rights Association, *Guyana Human Rights Report 1985* (Georgetown: Guyana Human Rights Association, 1985), pp. 8–9; "Criminal Horrors in Guyana," *Caribbean Contact* (October 1983), pp. 5–6; Tchaiko Kwayana, "Guyana: Nation Turned Upside Down," *Caribbean Contact* (September 1983), p. 14; "Criminal Gangs On Rampage," *Mirror*, November 17, 1985, p. 4; "Bandits Strike at Canal No. 1," *Catholic Standard*, May 12, 1985, p. 4; "Bandits Terrorise McDoom," *Catholic Standard*, September 29, 1985, p. 4; "Guyana: A land plagued by bandits," *Latin America Weekly Report*, April 26, 1983, pp. 9–10.

60. "Elections and Security Major Demands: WPA," *Catholic Standard*, August 4, 1985, p. 4.

61. "Guyana Politics: 'High Hopes' on US help," *Latin America Weekly Report*, June 26, 1986, p. 3.

62. Tchaiko Kwayana, "Guyana: Nation turned upside down," p. 14.

63. "Real Break With Past?," p. 2.

64. Guyana Human Rights Association, *Human Rights Report Jan. 1980-June 1981*, pp. 34, 64–65.

65. Lord Avebury and the British Parliamentary Human Rights Group, "Guyana's 1980 Elections: The Politics of Fraud," p. 9.

66. *Ibid.*, p. 10

67. Guyana Human Rights Association, *Human Rights Report Jan. 1980-June 1981*, p. 29.

68. "Why PPP Allowed Gift While *Standard* Denied," *Catholic Standard*, July 28, 1985, pp. 1, 4.

69. Guyana Human Rights Association, *Human Rights Report Jan. 1980-June 1981*, p. 30; Rickey Singh, "The Guyanese People have had enough of their prime minister's 'eye-pass'," *Caribbean Contact* (September 1979), p. 11.

70. "Growing o'seas support for Standard," *Catholic Standard*, November 25, 1984, p. 3.

71. "Cecil Griffith Editor of Stabroek News," *Catholic Standard*, November 9, 1986, p. 1; "The Impending Demise Of 'Stabroek News'?" *Caribbean Contact* (June 1987), p. 15.

72. "Death Of A Labour Movement," *Caribbean Contact* (April 1984), p. 1.

73. James Dastajir, "Crisis In The Labour Movement," *Thunder* 15 (April-June 1983), p. 32.

74. "Death Of A Labour Movement," p. 1.

75. "T.U.C. Warns Burnham: 'Enough'!" *Caribbean Contact* (December 1984), p. 2.

76. The World Bank, *Guyana: A Framework for Economic Recovery* (Washington, D.C.: The World Bank, 1984), p. 82.

77. Spinner, *A Political and Social History*, p. 202.

78. Kwayana, *Walter Rodney.* p. 12.

79. Jagan, *For a National Front Government*, p. 22. The author listened to the live radio broadcast of the proceedings at the rally on May Day, 1977.

80. Kwayana, *Walter Rodney*, p. 36.

81. Burnham, *Towards the People's Victory*, p. 14.

82. Kwayana, *Walter Rodney*, p. 38.

83. *Ibid.*

84. Dastajir, "Crisis In The Labour Movement," p. 32; "Beriberi Disease Brings Death and Fear Amid Guyana's Economic Crisis," *Caribbean Contact* (January 1983), p. 13.

85. "Guyana: Strikers challenge Burnham over food shortages," *Latin America Weekly Report*, June 17, 1983, p. 3; Terrence K. Millington, "Burnham hits USA in worsening crisis," *Caribbean Contact* (September 1983), p. 7; *National Unity For Democracy*, p. 63.

86. *National Unity For Democracy*, p. 64.

87. The World Bank, *Guyana*, p. 81.

88. *Ibid*, p. 146.

89. *National Unity For Democracy*, p. 64.

90. *Ibid*.

91. *Country Reports on Human Rights Practices for 1984: Report Submitted to the Committee on Foreign Relations, U.S. Senate and Committee on Foreign Affairs, U.S. House of Representatives by the Department of State* (Washington, D.C.: U.S. Government Printing Office, 1985), p. 562; "Guyana Labour: Wage rise softens devaluation blow," *Latin America Weekly Report*, February 12, 1987, p. 5.

92. *Country Reports on Human Rights Practices For 1984*, p. 563.

93. Guyana Human Rights Association, *Human Rights Report Jan. 1980-June 1981*, p. 38; "Priest Told To Leave Country," *Catholic Standard*, December 22, 1985, p. 1.

94. Hubert Williams, "The Great Church-State Row in Guyana: Government assurances versus pastors' fears," *Caribbean Contact* (October 1976), p. 8.

95. "Assault On Church: CCC Protests," *Caribbean Contact* (April 1985), p. 8.

96. "Bishops, Church Leaders' Homes Searched For Guns," *Catholic Standard*, December 22, 1985, p. 1.

97. Guyana Human Rights Association, *Human Rights Report Jan. 1980-June 1981*, pp. 45–48; *Country Human Rights Report for 1984*, pp. 565–566; Clive Thomas, "Collapse Of Guyana's Economy," *Caribbean Contact* (January 1982), p. 5; Tchaiko Kwayana, "Guyana: Nation turned upside down," *Caribbean Contact* (September 1983), p. 15; Terrence K. Millington, "Guyana: Grudging concessions but no solutions," *Caribbean Contact* (January/February, 1984), p. 11.

98. See Ranji Chandisingh, *Education In the Revolution For Socialist Transformation And Development* (Ruimveldt: Guyana Printers Ltd., 1979), pp. 26–28.

99. *Economic Liberation Through Socialism: Leader's Address–2nd Biennial Congress of the P.N.C.* (Ruimveldt: Guyana Printers Ltd., 1977), p. 24.

100. *Country Reports On Human Rights For 1985*, p. 566. See also Guyana Human Rights Association, *Guyana Human Rights Report 1985* (Georgetown: Guyana Human Rights Association, 1985), p. 37.

5

THE ECONOMY UNDER COOPERATIVE SOCIALISM

INTRODUCTION

The PNC first took office in December 1964 with a promise to usher in an era of prosperity. One of its election slogans was, "Free Cassava and Milk" for everyone. This was the Burnham equivalent of U.S. President Hoover's promise of "a chicken in every pot." However, in 1987, after 22 years in office, 17 of which have been under the regime of cooperative socialism, poverty rather than prosperity is in evidence everywhere. With a per capita GNP of U.S. $520 in 1983, Guyana ranks as one of the poorest countries in the Western Hemisphere.[1] The economy is in shambles. The country's export performance has been poor and its import capability severely impaired. The exchange rate for the Guyana dollar dropped from G$2.7 to U.S. $1.00 in the mid–1970s to G$4.4 to U.S. $1.00 by the end of 1986. Shortages of food and drugs are a basic fact of life. Diseases that were stamped out a long time ago have returned. There has been a proliferation of beggars. Most families are without milk, and until 1986, it was illegal to be in possession of bread. In order to conserve foreign exchange the government had banned the importation of wheat in 1982 and was encouraging Guyanese to consume rice instead. To enforce the flour ban, the courts were handing down stiff penalties to people in possession of bread or any other product made from flour. In fact, the penalty for the possession of bread was greater than for the possession of marijuana![2]

PLANNING DEVELOPMENT

As a colony, Guyana was an exporter of primary products. Until World War II, the economy rested essentially on sugar. However, after the war, bauxite and rice production became the other pillars of the economy. Revenues generated from taxing these exports were used to pay for the importation of fuel and manufactured goods, and food stuff. It was an economy that was subject to the vagaries of the international market for primary products. This was the colonial structure of economy, which the PNC inherited. And after over two decades of PNC management, the basic structure of the economy has not changed.

The slothfulness of economic development in Guyana has not been for a lack of planning. Even before the PNC made socialism its official ideology, it had drafted a development plan to chart its way to economic progress. Unfortunately, the PNC never took its development plans very seriously and the results differed enormously from the goals that were set. However, control over the election machinery gave the PNC a way of eluding public chastisement for its economic failures.

The first PNC development plan was for the seven-year period, 1966–1972.[3] Like many other Commonwealth Caribbean countries, the Burnham regime followed a policy popularly known as "industrialization by invitation," the basic premise of which was that industrialization would result from foreign investment and, therefore, all the government had to do was to make the country attractive to foreign investors. In order to do this, the Burnham regime concentrated its efforts on infrastructural development such as the improvement of roads, harbor facilities, transportation and communication systems, drainage and irrigation, and electricity generation. However, the foreign investors that were so crucial to the success of this developmental thrust did not go to Guyana. In any case, the Burnham regime abandoned this development plan in 1970, when it declared that cooperative socialism would be its ideology and its development strategy.

The second PNC development plan was announced in 1972, though it was not put into operation until 1973. The 1972–1976 development plan intended to make the cooperative sector the dominant sector of the economy.[4] By means of this five-year plan, the Burnham regime hoped to make Guyana self-sufficient in several basic areas by 1976. The domestic slogan, which was posted as a greeting sign at the entrance of every town and every village, read "Feed, Clothe, And House The Nation By 1976." However, by 1976, the cooperative sector was still a floundering experiment, and the FCH program, as it was referred to, never realistically approached the stated objectives. The most important development during this period was the increase in government control over the economy. By the end of 1976, the government directly controlled 80 percent of the economy, including the bauxite and sugar industries.

The development plans discussed above were similar in two respects. First, in neither of these plans was the domestic private sector assigned any important role in the development effort. Even the 1966–1972 development plan, which held out an open invitation to international capital, treated the domestic private sector by omission. On the other hand, the pace of nationalization and the accompanying socialist rhetoric sent alarm through the private sector and resulted in capital flight. The second observation concerns the implementation of the plans. The government's annual budgets did not consistently reflect the goals outlined in the development plans. The result was that the plans were simply not implemented.[5] This tendency on the part of the government to ignore its development plan has prompted one commentator to observe that the government appeared to be more concerned with constructing plans for publication than for implementation.[6]

The only other development plan put forth by the PNC covered the 1978–1982 period. This plan was launched with much less fanfare than its predecessors. The stated goal was to achieve a socialist society, one characterized by "the creation of wealth under humane conditions and the just and equitable distribution of that wealth."[7] In 1982, however, Guyana had become a poverty-stricken society. The admission of failure for another development plan was made by the finance minister when he said, "We survived 1982—and that was a great achievement."[8]

PERFORMANCE OF THE ECONOMY UNDER STATE CONTROL

The data tend to support the assertion by critics of the PNC that the regime has been far more successful at managing the country's elections than it has been at managing the economy. As Table 5.1 shows, national output has been declining since 1977. Except for 1980, the economy has experienced a negative growth rate for every year from 1977 to 1983. Guyana is not expected to reattain its 1975 level of GDP before 1990.[9]

As Table 5.2 shows, the performance of two pillars of the economy—bauxite and sugar—has been less than spectacular. Bauxite production has consistently declined after 1976. Sugar production has fluctuated considerably since 1976 but has remained below the 1976 level of production. Rice production has also fluctuated after 1977 and has yet to reattain the 1977 level of production. Exports of all of these commodities have been declining (see Table 5.3). Export earnings have not been sufficient to cover imports, despite efforts to compress the level of imports by eliminating certain consumption items (see Table 5.4).

Guyana has incurred balance of payments deficits in every year since 1976, and the government has engaged in extensive external borrowing. The result is that Guyana has accumulated an external debt which, in 1984, stood at U.S. $1.23 billion. Guyana's largest creditor is the International Monetary Fund (IMF). In 1985, the debt payment due to the IMF was U.S. $31.7 million, or approximately 41 percent of Guyana's export earnings for that year, which Guyana could not afford to pay.[10] Because of its inability to meet its international financial obligations, Guyana has been classified as "not creditworthy for non-concessional financing."[11]

Table 5.1
Gross Domestic Product (GDP) at Constant Factor Cost, 1970–1984 (G$ Million - 1977 prices)

YEAR	GDP
1970	854
1971	884
1972	852
1973	872
1974	941
1975	1,032
1976	1,050
1977	1,019
1978	990
1979	976
1980	992
1981	989
1982	886
1983	801
1984	845

Source: The World Bank, Guyana: A Framework for Economic Recovery, p. 85.

Guyana has been experiencing a severe shortage of foreign currency. At the end of 1984, Guyana's foreign exchange reserves amounted to *negative* U.S. $663.4 million.[12] The lack of foreign exchange has severely constricted the government's ability to import consumption goods, as well as inputs for production. Shortages of previously imported consumer goods, including basic food items, have had a profound impact on the general health and welfare of the population, and a thriving parallel market has developed. The parallel market has become the largest market for foreign exchange, gold and diamonds, and "in certain basic consumer items like cheese and butter, coffee, flour and so on, some canned and processed foods—it is probably the largest market within the country."[13]

Shortage of foreign exchange has also adversely affected state-owned

Table 5.2
Output of Bauxite, Sugar, Rice, 1974–1984 (Thousands of long tons)

Year	Dried Bauxite	Calcined Bauxite	Alumina*	Sugar	Rice
1974	1,383.0	726.0	311.0	340.8	153.3
1975	1,350.0	778.0	294.0	300.4	60.0
1976	969.0	729.0	265.0	322.5	110.0
1977	879.0	709.0	273.0	241.5	211.5
1978	1,021.9	570.0	236.0	324.8	182.0
1979	1,058.5	568.0	159.7	298.3	142.8
1980	1,005.5	591.6	211.5	269.6	166.4
1981	982.0	505.4	167.1	300.8	163.0
1982	958.0	385.0	93.0	287.0	179.0
1983	761.0	310.0	-----	251.8	147.6
1984	823.0	517.0	-----	237.9	181.1

Note: *Alumina production ceased in 1982.

Source: The World Bank, *Guyana: A Framework for Economic Recovery*, pp. 144–145

industries, which have not been able to obtain spare parts to refurbish their plant and equipment, and this has resulted in an enormous amount of unused capacity and lower production. The government has used barter arrangements to obtain some Eastern bloc goods. While the terms of the arrangements have not been made public, the circumstances under which the Guyana government entered into these agreements were so desperate that the government had to have settled for less than it ordinarily would have. The principal commodity used in these barter arrangements was bauxite, and, as discussed later in this chapter, unreliability as a supplier was costing Guyana some of its international customers. Barter agreements, therefore, became substitutes for more lucrative markets.

State control of the economy is unquestionably the principal explanatory variable behind the protracted economic malaise afflicting Guyana. The public sector is large and unwieldy. Through nationalizations, the regime has enlarged its direct control over the economy. The government has estimated the percentage of the economy under its direct control to be 80 percent. The government also exercises indirect control over all

Table 5.3
Exports of Bauxite, Sugar, Rice, 1974–1984 (Thousands of long tons)

Year	Dried Bauxite	Calcined Bauxite	Alumina	Sugar	Rice
1974	1,338.0	767.0	302.0	302.4	51.0
1975	1,363.0	772.0	320.0	285.0	82.0
1976	825.0	731.0	265.0	297.0	71.0
1977	882.0	693.0	263.0	207.7	65.9
1978	999.0	578.0	248.0	280.7	104.8
1979	1,010.8	542.3	145.0	264.2	83.7
1980	998.0	593.5	226.0	248.1	79.7
1981	995.1	488.2	149.6	264.6	76.8
1982	692.0	365.0	64.0	250.2	34.3
1983	821.0	319.0	29.0	213.2	41.7
1984	823.0	501.0	-----	201.1	46.7

Source: The World Bank, *Guyana: A Framework for Economic Recovery*, pp. 144–145.

other economic enterprises through its control over licensing arrangements and through its control over the allocation of scarce foreign exchange. Imports are also controlled by the government through the Guyana National Trading Corporation (GNTC).

Since the mid–1970s, the PNC government has been incurring large budget deficits. Until 1981, it was able to offset these deficits by the surpluses of the public corporations. However, since 1981, the public corporations have been incurring large operating deficits. The result has been a widening of the overall deficit. Whereas, in 1978, the deficit amounted to 13 percent of the gross domestic product, in 1984, it had amounted to 60 percent of the gross domestic product. The government has been financing the overall deficit by borrowing.[14] In 1984, the finance charges for the internal debt exceeded government revenues for that year.[15]

THE THREE PILLARS OF THE ECONOMY

The Bauxite Industry

Guyana is reputedly rich in minerals, including gold and diamonds. The exploitation of this mineral wealth has been impeded by the fact

Table 5.4
Foreign Trade (U.S.$ million)

Year	Exports	Imports	Balance
1973	135.4	175.1	−39.7
1974	270.2	254.4	15.8
1975	364.4	344.1	20.3
1976	279.2	363.6	−84.4
1977	259.3	315.4	−56.1
1978	295.5	278.9	16.6
1979	291.3	317.7	−26.4
1980	388.9	396.1	− 7.2
1981	346.4	439.6	−93.2
1982	242.2	280.4	−38.2
1983	189.0	230.3	−41.3

Source: The World Bank, *Guyana: A Framework For Economic Recovery*, p. 95. United Nations, *1985 International Trade Statistics Yearbook, Volume I* (New York: United Nations, 1987), p. 467.

that the minerals are located in the region that is the center of a border dispute between Guyana and Venezuela. Oil exploration is being conducted in Guyana on the assumption that the country's juxtaposition to Venezuela and Trinidad, both of which are oil producers, might hold some promise of Guyana becoming a producer also. As of August 1987, oil has not been found in commercial quantities. The production of precious metals has been far below potential. Between 1980 and 1984, declared gold production averaged approximately 11,100 ounces annually, and diamond production averaged 10,000 carats.[16] These figures understate the true production because the parallel market plays an important role in the trading of precious metals. With more sophisticated production techniques, the level of gold production could be elevated to 375,000 ounces annually and that of diamond production to 700,000 carats annually.[17] In May 1987, President Hoyte announced that his government had given out licenses to foreign companies in an effort to increase the production of these precious metals.[18]

Bauxite production dominates the mining industry in Guyana. Bauxite mining operations began in Guyana in 1914, but the most rapid development took place after World War II. Before government intervention in the industry, two foreign companies controlled the bauxite industry. The larger company was the Demerara Bauxite Company (DEMBA), whose operations were centered at Linden, and the smaller company was Reynolds Bauxite Company, whose operations were centered at Kwakwani. The Burnham regime had not originally intended to take over the bauxite industry entirely. Responding to clamor within his own party that the country should have a greater share of the bauxite revenues, Burnham demanded majority participation in DEMBA. When the company resisted, the government passed the enabling legislation and nationalized the company in 1971. DEMBA's assets were vested in the newly-formed Guyana Bauxite Company (GUYBAU). Thereafter, the nationalization of Reynolds seemed inevitable. In 1974, the Burnham government, reassured by its brief experience with the GUYBAU operations, succumbed to nationalist pressures within the PNC and also from the PPP and nationalized Reynolds Bauxite Company. The government created the Berbice Mining Enterprise (BERMINE) to take over the assets of Reynolds. The two state-owned bauxite companies were later merged for administrative purposes and the entire bauxite industry is now run by the Guyana Mining Enterprise (GUYMINE).

Under state control, bauxite production has been steadily decreasing. In fact, the industry has been incurring losses in its operations.[19] The reasons for this situation in the bauxite industry are myriad. At the time of nationalization, Guyana did not have the technological and managerial skills necessary to run the bauxite industry on a profitable basis. This became very clear after 1975 when production began to fall. The PNC also integrated the bauxite industry into its patronage system, and used the high-paying positions in GUYMINE to reward party loyals. Political criteria rather than managerial expertise determined appointments, promotions, and company decisions. Another consequence of political patronage was an overly inflated work force in the bauxite industry, though under pressure from the IMF, but also for punitive purposes, the PNC government reduced the work force by about one-third in 1983. PNC interference in the activities of the bauxite union caused labor relations in the industry to be very tense, but grievances over wages and shortages were also contributory factors to poor labor relations.

Plants and equipment in the industry have not been kept in good repair and this has resulted in low capacity utilization. The industry also has problems in the marketing of its output. Declining quality and a low reputation for reliability caused a reduction in Guyana's share of the market for calcined bauxite from about 80 percent in the 1960s and 1970s to 50 percent in the 1980s.[20] Unless the government can resolve these problems, Guyana could be reduced to the status of a supplier of last resort. The government has been trying to rehabilitate the bauxite industry by using foreign consultants. The most recent negotiations have been with Reynolds Metals Company.[21]

The Sugar Industry

The sugar industry is the oldest industry in Guyana. As discussed in Chapter 1, it was the sugar industry that determined the settlement pattern in Guyana. Up through the 1950s, sugar dominated the economy of Guyana and was closely associated with British rule. Even though the sugar companies had made tremendous strides in terms of employing locals at all levels of management, a national consensus developed regarding the need to nationalize the sugar industry.

Nationalization of the sugar industry took place in two stages. The smaller company, Jessel Securities Ltd., was nationalized in 1975, and the larger company, Booker Brothers McConnell & Co. Ltd., was nationalized in 1976. The government created the Guyana Sugar Corporation (GUYSUCO) to run the nationalized companies. There has been little change in the organization of the sugar industry under GUYSUCO's control. The industry is still operated on a plantation basis with a very large labor force. The bulk of the sugar cane needs of the industry is produced on GUYSUCO's sugar estates, though independent small farmers are able to earn a comfortable living from supplying sugar cane to GUYSUCO. The principal products of the industry are crude sugar crystals (brown sugar), molasses, and rum.

Guyana markets 200,000 tons of sugar annually to the European Economic Community under a protective arrangement. The rest of its export is sold in the world market. However, the world market price for sugar has been declining since 1976, and this has adversely affected the foreign exchange earnings of the sugar industry.[22] The general shortage of foreign exchange has affected the industry's ability to acquire desperately needed spare parts.

The sugar industry is plagued by industrial unrest. In 1984 alone, there were 480 strikes in the sugar industry, involving a loss of 152,000 man-days.[23] The sugar workers are organized into two unions, the Guyana Agricultural Workers' Union (GAWU), and the National Association of Agricultural, Clerical and Industrial Employees (NAACIE). GAWU is the larger union and is controlled by the PPP. NAACIE is a much more independent union, but it is very sympathetic to the PPP. The PPP uses its control over the work force in the sugar industry to apply pressure on the government. Not only are strikes frequent in the sugar industry, they can also be very protracted. The 1977 sugar workers' strike lasted 125 days. Although the sugar industry has been the principal foreign exchange earner in recent years, the sugar workers, particularly those who cut the sugar cane, are among the lowest paid category of workers in the country. Industrial grievances are, therefore, not difficult to find to justify strikes whose real purposes might be more political.

Partly in response to deteriorating market conditions for sugar, GUY-SUCO began to reduce the acreage under sugar cultivation. In 1986, the sugar estate at Leonora was closed and, in 1987, the sugar estate at Diamond was closed. Only eight sugar estates remain in operation. The state corporation plans to reduce the land under sugar cane cultivation from 120,000 acres to 90,000 acres. The land freed up from sugar production will be used for dairy farming, aquaculture, and to raise other crops such as rice, root crops, and orchard crops.[24]

The Rice Industry

Rice has been grown in Guyana since the eighteenth century. However, the rice industry was built up to the status of an export industry by Indian farmers. While there are also black rice farmers in Guyana, the overwhelming majority of the rice farmers are Indians. The PNC has been persistent in its attempts to get blacks to take up farming, but appeals such as the "Land is the Mother of our existence" appeal have not succeeded in bringing blacks into large-scale farming.[25]

Rice is grown on small and medium farms along the coast of Guyana. The industry is very mechanized. Plows are tractor-drawn and, except in a small number of cases, mechanical harvesters are used to reap the crops. The rice mills are modern and are privately owned but are closely monitored by the government. The government is the sole marketer of rice. The government exercises this function through the Guyana Rice Board. The farmers are required to sell their paddy to the Rice Board at prices fixed by the government. The paddy is then milled and the rice is turned over to the Board for export and for domestic distribution. Since the government banned the importation of wheat flour in 1978, the domestic demand for rice has risen. However, because of the pressure for foreign exchange, the government exports the bulk of the milled rice. The result is that severe shortages of this staple are frequent in Guyana and are part of the general food shortage in the country.

The monopoly role of the Guyana Rice Board has been a major part of the problem with the rice industry. The members of the Board are all appointed by the government. The Rice Producers' Association does not have any representation on the Rice Board. Party loyalty rather than knowledge of the rice industry is the criterion for appointment. Farmers complain that the Board does not understand, and is not sympathetic, to their problems. Farmers complain bitterly about being cheated by the Rice Board in the weighing and grading of their grain.[26] Rice farmers have not been able to get spare parts for their farm machinery, and devaluations of the Guyana currency plus high import duties on farm

Table 5.5
Consumer Price Indices (Urban) (1970 = 100)

Year	Composite Index
1970	100.0
1971	101.0
1972	106.0
1973	114.0
1974	134.0
1975	144.0
1976	157.6
1977	170.7
1978	196.5
1979	231.4
1980	264.0
1981	322.7
1982	390.2
1983	448.7

Source: The World Bank, Guyana: A Framework For Economic Recovery, p. 146.

machinery make new purchases prohibitive. The result of all of this has been low morale among rice farmers, and those who can emigrate. Morale dipped to a new low with the passage of the 1985 Rice Act that empowers the Rice Board to enter the premises of farmers to search for paddy and rice.[27]

THE QUALITY OF LIFE UNDER COOPERATIVE SOCIALISM

As Table 5.5 of consumer price indices shows, the cost of living sky-rocketed after 1973, with the greatest increases occurring over the period 1978–1983, when the government was engaged in massive retrenchment in the public sector. Unemployment in Guyana at the end of 1986 was at least 30 percent.[28]

The quality of life in Guyana has plummeted under PNC rule. There are recurrent food shortages.[29] In an effort to conserve foreign exchange, the regime banned the importation of many basic food items such as wheat flour, cheese, garlic, and onions, for which there are no local substitutes. Until late 1986, rice, in some form, was consumed at every meal, but because of the regime's push to acquire foreign exchange, there were shortages of rice in the domestic market. Food items that are available are distributed by party controlled outlets, and there have been allegations from church groups that available food is distributed in a discriminatory manner. The waiting lines for food items are interminable, and in some cases, are formed overnight. People absent themselves from work to position themselves in food lines. Absence from work and the lack of proper nutrition have had a deleterious effect on productivity, and food demands have been a key issue in the frequent strikes and demonstrations.

There has also been a marked deterioration in the provision of basic utilities. All of the utilities in Guyana are government-owned. Electrical blackouts are frequent and protracted. The water and sewage systems are not properly maintained; the available drinking water is discolored and is a health hazard, and may in fact be the cause of the frequent cases of gastroenteritis. There are frequent breakdowns in the sewage system. The health risks from these are magnified by the only intermittent availability of soap.[30]

Diseases that had once been eradicated from Guyana have reappeared in epidemic proportion. These include beriberi, malaria, and scabies. Malnutrition has also increased and its toll on children has been particularly severe. In 1984, 71 percent of all children under five years old had confirmed symptoms of malnutrition.[31] The infant mortality rate in 1981 was 42.7 per 1,000 live births.[32]

There has also been a deterioration in the provision of health care. Almost all of the hospitals are government-owned and operated, and all are in poor physical repair. Space and beds are inadequate, and two patients share a bed. This is even the case in the maternity wards.[33] There is a shortage of medical personnel. In 1970, the population per physician was 4,250, while in 1979, it had risen to 9,270.[34] Many Guyanese doctors have emigrated, and the majority of the doctors in Guyana today are foreigners. There are also shortages of drugs. The decline in the quality of health care, especially when there is an increase in the need for such care, has been taking a very heavy toll on the population.

Conditions of life were so horrible in Guyana in 1983 that in his 1984 New Year's Day speech Burnham admitted that "only the Will to Survive kept us going,"[35] and in presenting the 1984 budget, Finance Minister Carl Greenidge said, "I can offer no comforting solution which will allow us to survive and prosper."[36]

While the broad mass of Guyanese were suffering these hardships and were being called on to make more sacrifices, their "functional superiors," as members of the PNC elite refer to themselves, were engaged in ostentatious living. The minimum wage in Guyana in 1984 was G$15.10 per day, about the price of a pint of cooking oil.[37] The official exchange rate was G$4.3 per U.S. dollars. However, the parallel market rate was about G$18.00 per U.S. dollar.[38] Hence, in real terms, the minimum daily wage in Guyana was less than U.S. $1.00. The regime strongly resisted demands for an increase in the minimum daily wage. However, in January 1985, the regime voted huge retroactive increases for senior government officials. The president's annual salary increased from G$31,000 to G$66,000, an increase of 109 percent. The prime minister's salary increased from G$24,000 to G$60,000, an increase of 150 percent. The vice-presidents each received an increase of 121 percent. Senior ministers and regular ministers received increases of 94.4 percent and 66.6 percent respectively. All increases, except the president's, were retroactive from January 1984. The president's was retroactive from July 1984.[39] In addition, the Office of the General Secretary of the PNC, which is merged with the Ministry of National Development, continues to provide the ruling party with a direct tap into the public treasury. The frequent Guyanese complaint that " 'thiefing' is the no. 1 industry in Guyana," is meant to apply both to officialdom and to the proliferation of armed bandits.

The deteriorating quality of life in Guyana and the repression with which the ruling party maintains itself in power have caused an exodus from the country. Guyana loses approximately 1 percent of its population per year through out-migration.[40] The United States, Canada, Trinidad, and Surinam are the principal receiving countries. Many Guyanese are awaiting sponsorships by relatives living overseas, which will permit them to emigrate. Emigration has become a mentality in Guyana in the sense that there is a feeling on the part of many that the suffering need only be endured pending the processing of their emigration documents. Many of those who remain in Guyana are aided, in their struggle to survive, by financial remittances and barrels of food from relatives overseas.

In reviewing the economic conditions in Guyana over the past decade, one is led to the inescapable conclusion that cooperative socialism has been a dramatic and costly failure. It has reduced the country to utter prostration. Rather than giving the people maximum participation in their economic lives, it has increasingly centralized economic decision making, to the detriment of the economic well-being of the population. National morale is low. There are few incentives to produce. The people vote with their feet, and in so doing, affix a resounding judgment of failure on cooperative socialism.

A NEW DIRECTION

In late 1986, the Hoyte administration reintroduced wheat flour into Guyana through a PL 480 agreement signed with the United States. The agreement was renewed in 1987. The move, which undid the Burnham ban on this Guyanese staple, raised expectations of even greater economic relief. These expectations were shattered in January 1987 when the finance minister announced in his budget speech that the Guyana dollar was to be devalued by 127 percent, from G$4.40 to U.S. $1.00 to a rate of G$10.00 to U.S. $1.00. The devaluation was inevitable given that the exchange rate in the parallel market had climbed to about G$20.00 to U.S. $1.00, a clear indication that the Guyana currency was overvalued. The devaluation was also part of an effort to effect a contraction of the parallel market. The other part of the plan included a decision by the government to operate "special windows" at all banks to buy foreign exchange at rates comparable to those in the parallel market. The government promised that these would be "no-questions-asked" transactions.

Nevertheless, the massive devaluation of the Guyana dollar in January 1987, signaled more hardships for an already severely strapped population and inspired the resurrection of an old calypso entitled, "Ten to One is Murder." The government promised to take measures to cushion the likely effects on the population, but the WPA's Eusi Kwayana dismissed the measures as "nothing but leaking life-belts," and the leader of the PPP said that the new budget "will impose hardships never before experienced by the people."[41]

What became clear from the finance minister's budget presentation was the fact that the government was embarking on an entirely new economic course. The minister made it clear that the government intended to dismantle all legislative obstacles to foreign investment and to provide adequate protection for such investment.[42] The government has since that time opened up considerably to the local private sector. As President Hoyte said in his 1987 May Day speech, his government "unapologetically will continue to support and give every assistance to private sector activities in this country."[43] In his determination to "fix the economy," Hoyte has turned to free enterprise, a move that has generated greater optimism within a population that has grown tired of socialist rhetoric and its seemingly unending demand for sacrifices. In 1987, the government has not publicly talked about cooperatives or cooperative socialism. It is ironic, indeed, that the cooperative is likely to find its grave in the world's only cooperative republic.

NOTES

1. "Country Data," in the World Bank, *Guyana: A Framework for Economic Recovery* (Washington, D.C.: The World Bank, 1985), p. 1.

2. Terrence K. Millington, "Celebration of a party's victory over Guyanese people," *Caribbean Contact* (May 1983), p. 7.

3. See *The ABC of the 1966–1972 Development Programme* (Georgetown: The Daily Chronicle Ltd., undated); and *The Great Advance in Infrastructure Development Under the P.N.C. Government, Address by Desmond Hoyte, Minister of Works and Communications at the 16th Annual Delegates' Congress of the People's National Congress, May 2–10, 1973*.

4. Kempe R. Hope, *The Post-War Planning Experience in Guyana* (Tempe, Arizona: Center for Latin American Studies, Arizona State University, 1978), pp. 26–28.

5. *Ibid.*, p. 24.

6. *Ibid.*

7. "A Socialist Economy through Agricultural, Industrial and Technological Development," paper presented by Cde. Desmond Hoyte, Member of the General Council and of the Central Executive Committee, P.N.C. Legal Advisor to the General Secretary, P.N.C., and Minister of Economic Development and Cooperatives at the 3rd Biennial Congress of the People's National Congress, held at Sophia, Georgetown, from 22nd to 26th August, 1979.

8. Minister of Finance, *Budget 1983* (Georgetown: Ministry of Finance, 1983), p. 25.

9. The World Bank, *Guyana*, p. v.

10. Carl B. Greenidge, *Budget 1985: Developing Within Our Means* (Ruimveldt: Guyana National Printers Ltd., 1985), pp. 51, 83.

11. The World Bank, *Guyana*, p. ii.

12. *Ibid.*, p. 138.

13. Clive Thomas, *Hoyte's Economic Dynamism: Can It Work?* (Georgetown: Working People's Alliance, 1986). p. 8.

14. Greenidge, *Budget 1985*, pp. 75–76; The World Bank, *Guyana*, p. i.

15. *National Unity For Democracy*, p. 34.

16. The World Bank, *Guyana*, p. 145.

17. *Ibid.*

18. *Address By His Excellency Cde. H.D. Hoyte, S.C., President of the Co-operative Republic of Guyana To The May Day Rally At The National Park On May 1, 1987* (No other publication information), p. 12.

19. The World Bank, *Guyana*, pp. 17–20. See also Clive Thomas, "Collapse of Guyana's Economy," *Caribbean Contact* (January 1982), p. 5.

20. The World Bank, *Guyana*, p. 18.

21. "Contract With Reynolds Being Re-Negotiated," *Catholic Standard*, October 27, 1985, p. 1.

22. For prices of sugar imports into the United States, see U.S. Department of Commerce, *Statistical Abstract of the United States 1979* (Washington, D.C.: U.S. Government Printing Office, 1979), p. 4812; U.S. Department of Commerce, *Statistical Abstract of the United States 1985* (Washington, D.C.: U.S. Government Printing Office, 1984), p. 473.

23. The World Bank, *Guyana*, p. 82.

24. "Guyana, Economy: Moving away from sugar," *Latin America Weekly Report*, February 26, 1987, p. 10; "Sugar Industry Considers Further Diversification," *Viewpoint* (May 1987), p. 2; *Address By His Excellency, Cde. H.D. Hoyte. S.C.*, p. 12.

25. "A Socialist Economy through Agricultural, Industrial and Technical Development," p. 18.

26. "Rice Industry In Crisis," *Catholic Standard*, August 4, 1985, p. 1; "Rice Producers Want More Say," *Catholic Standard*, September 29, 1985, p. 2.

27. "New Rice Bill Tightens Govt. Control of Rice Industry," *Catholic Standard*, December 23, 1984, p. 5.

28. No official figure for unemployment has been made public. See "Guyana's Devaluation Gloom," *Caribbean Contact* (May 1987), p. 16.

29. *Country Reports On Human Rights Practices for 1983*, p. 597; Terrence K. Millington, "Guyana: Grudging Concessions but no solutions," *Caribbean Contact* (January/February 1984), p. 11; the Guyana Human Rights Association, *Guyana Human Rights Report 1985*, pp. 9–13.

30. *Country Reports on Human Rights Practices for 1984*, p. 565; Millington, "Guyana: Grudging Concessions but no solutions," p. 11.

31. The Guyana Human Rights Association, *Guyana Human Rights Report 1985*, p. 36.

32. The World Bank, *World Tables* (Baltimore: The Johns Hopkins University Press, 1983), p. 39.

33. "Two-In-A-Bed At PHG," *Mirror*, November 17, 1985, p. 4.

34. The World Bank, *World Tables*, p. 39.

35. *New Year Message To The Nation By Cde. L. F. S. Burnham, O.E., S.C., President of the Co-operative Republic of Guyana, 1984* (Georgetown: Office of the President, 1984), p. 1.

36. Carl B. Greenidge, *1984 Budget* (Georgetown: Ministry of Finance and Economic Planning, 1984), p. 78.

37. The Guyana Human Rights Association, *Guyana Human Rights Report 1985*, p. 34.

38. "The US dollar in Latin America & the Caribbean," *Latin American Weekly Report*, July 13, 1986, p. 11.

39. "Cake for elite, crumbs for workers," *Mirror*, January 20, 1985, p.1. See also, The Guyana Human Rights Association, *Guyana Human Rights Report 1985*, p. 34.

40. The World Bank, *Guyana*, p. 80.

41. "Ten to One Devaluation," *Caribbean Contact* (February 1987), p. 10.

42. "Guyana Deemphasizes Socialism," *Caribbean Monitor* (March 1987), p. 9.

43. *Address By His Excellency. Cde. H. D. Hoyte. S.C.*, p 12.

6

FOREIGN RELATIONS

INTRODUCTION

Although Guyana is a South American country, it has remained relatively isolated from its Latin neighbors. Indeed, until 1962 when Venezuela reactivated its territorial claim against Guyana, the latter had had little official contact with other South American countries. Guyana's relative isolation on the continent can be explained by its distinctive colonial experience. It was the only British colony in South America, and it is today the only English-speaking country in the continent. Its colonial status ended in 1966, but until that time, Guyana's principal external contacts were with Britain and other British territories, particularly those in the Caribbean. Historically and culturally, Guyana has far greater similarities with, and affinities to, the Commonwealth Caribbean than it does with its Latin neighbors.

Within Guyana, some have argued that the country's mainland location sets it apart from the other Commonwealth Caribbean countries and that Guyana should follow its continental destiny. The implication here is that Guyana's future might be more closely linked to that of the other South American countries. This position is an attractive one, especially since in developmental terms, several of the Latin countries rank among the most developed of the Third World and presumably Guyana can benefit from closer association with them. As of August 1987, there have been no significant moves in this direction. While Guyana has supported the positions taken by Latin American countries on various international issues, serious bilateral relations have been confined to its immediate neighbors, Venezuela and Brazil, and have not produced the kind of results that would encourage Guyana to intensify its links with the rest of the continent.

Guyana has instead opted for wider links with the Third World. Guyana has also remained within the British-led Commonwealth, though relations between the governments of Guyana and Britain have not been especially close. Finally, the Guyana government has always been aware of the fact that it must operate in a hemisphere dominated by the United States. To a government that has embraced a socialist ideology, this recognition can be very worrisome.

RELATIONS WITH THE UNITED STATES

The United States was very generous to the Burnham government during its first term in office. In 1965 alone, U.S. loans and grants to Guyana totalled U.S. $12.3 million compared to U.S. $4.9 million given to the Jagan government over the eight-year period 1957 to 1964. For the next three years, U.S. aid to the Burnham government averaged U.S. $8.6 million per year.[1]

Burnham, for his part, tried to reassure the United States of the pro-Western orientation of his government. At home, he reaffirmed his dedication to pluralist democracy and called his particular version, consultative democracy. He declared that his government would never permit the establishment of any military base that posed a threat to Guyana's neighbors or to any country in the hemisphere. Additionally, he terminated Guyana's lucrative rice contract with Cuba.[2]

Relations between the United States and Guyana began to cool after 1969. After the PNC's victory in the 1968 election, the Burnham government received U.S. $17.6 million in aid from the United States. However, U.S. aid to Guyana dropped precipitously after 1969.[3] There are two plausible explanations for this decrease in aid. First, the Burnham victory in the 1968 election seemed to have convinced the United States that the threat posed by Marxist Cheddi Jagan had been contained. To the extent that U.S. aid to the Burnham government was a reaction to this threat, the United States now had little incentive to continue such a high per capita aid program. Second, after 1969, Burnham began to execute an ideological about-face. He described himself as a socialist and, in 1970, cooperative socialism became the government's development strategy. The decline in U.S. aid was a clear indication that the United States was not going to subsidize a socialist experiment.

Following its espousal of cooperative socialism, the Burnham government embarked on a spate of nationalizations that included Reynolds Bauxite Company, the Guyana subsidiary of Reynolds Metals Company of the United States. These nationalizations were a breach of the assurance given by Burnham to the United States government that private investment would be promoted and protected.[4] The government also established and enlarged relations with communist countries. In December 1972, Guyana established diplomatic relations with Cuba. Regular air service between Georgetown and Havana was restored. In August 1973, Fidel Castro made a state visit to Guyana, an event that greatly boosted Burnham's socialist image. One month later, Burnham flew with

Castro and Jamaica's Michael Manley, in Castro's plane, to the Non-Aligned Conference in Algiers. In April 1975, Burnham traveled to Havana where he was granted Cuba's highest award, the José Martí award. After that visit, the two countries exchanged resident ambassadors, and trade and aid ties expanded.[5] In particular, the Cubans undertook to supply medical personnel to Guyana, to train Guyanese to become doctors, and to provide assistance to Guyana's fishing industry.

Cuban influence was also apparent in Guyana's domestic politics. Castro was instrumental in forging a rapprochement between Forbes Burnham and Cheddi Jagan, both of whom had been in Cuba in 1975. Cuban representatives were present at both the PPP's 25th anniversary conference and the first biennial congress of the PNC. At the 25th anniversary conference of the PPP, Jagan announced a policy of "critical support" for the PNC government. The PPP's new policy helped pave the way for closer ties between the Burnham government, on the one hand, and Cuba and the Soviet Union, on the other. As Manley correctly observes, the PPP has had a long-standing friendship with both Cuba and the Soviet Union and close ties between Burnham and these countries were unlikely as long as the PPP remained adamant in its criticism of Burnham and the PNC. The PPP's policy of critical support removed this obstacle. In fact, in February 1976, the Soviet Union appointed a resident ambassador to Georgetown.[6]

Guyana's ties with other communist countries were also increased over this period. Between 1972 and 1975, China made interest-free loans to Guyana amounting to G$74 million. Burnham visited China in March 1975. The Chinese agreed to purchase a variety of Guyanese commodities, including bauxite, sugar, and timber. The Chinese assisted in the construction of a clay brick factory, a textile factory, and a 200-bed hospital in Guyana. Eastern European countries concluded similar trade agreements with Guyana. East Germany signed a long-term trade agreement with Guyana, under which it would purchase substantial amounts of bauxite and alumina. Guyana would, in return, buy machinery, electrical, and pharmaceutical commodities from East Germany. Hungary also agreed to buy Guyana's bauxite. Technical assistance of various types was promised by Poland, Czechoslovakia, and Yugoslavia.[7]

The narrowing of the ideological gap between the PNC and the PPP, the continued moves by the PNC government toward national ownership of foreign companies, and the increasingly friendly ties set up with communist countries provided reasons for concern to the United States. One indication of U.S. displeasure with these developments was the meager amount of foreign aid provided to Guyana during this period. However, the verbal exchanges between the two governments became very acrimonious during 1976. In January 1976, the United States government accused the Burnham government of permitting Guyana's Timehri Airport to be used for refueling purposes by Cuban military aircraft en route to Angola. Articles in the Brazilian newspaper, *Estado De Sao Paulo* and in the Venezuelan magazine, *Resumen*, alleged that there were thousands of Cuban and Chinese troops in Guyana. There were rumors that Venezuela and Brazil were conducting military maneuvers on Guyana's borders. The feeling in Guyana was that an invasion was imminent, though none took place. Guyana's foreign minister, Fred Wills, complained at the Non-Aligned Conference in Algiers, that there was a concerted attempt to destabilize the government of Guyana.[8]

Relations between the Burnham government and the United States deteriorated even further during the fall of 1976. On October 6, an Air Cubana plane, which had made a stop in Guyana, was blown up off the coast of Barbados. Among the 73 people who died were 11 Guyanese, six of whom were going to Cuba to study medicine. Both Fidel Castro and Forbes Burnham linked the CIA with the disaster, and Burnham named an official of the U.S. Embassy in Caracas, Venezuela, as a conspirator in the crime. Burnham saw the bombing of the plane as part of a "conspiracy against progressive Caribbean governments, particularly Cuba and Guyana."[9] The U.S. State Department responded to the charges by accusing Burnham of engaging in "bold-faced lies."[10] The United States also recalled its ambassador from Georgetown.

Relations between Guyana and the United States remained very tense for the remainder of President Ford's term but improved somewhat after Jimmy Carter took office. In August 1977, U.S. Ambassador to the U.N., Andrew Young, made a tour of the Caribbean, which included a stopover in Guyana. His message seemed to be that there really was a change in Washington and that the region's leaders could expect more sympathetic understanding.[11] Other senior U.S. officials were echoing the same theme. Commenting on the socialist path espoused by the Guyana government, the Assistant Secretary of State for Inter-American Affairs, Terrence Todman, said, "Guyana is seeking a different path to social and economic development, one with which we have no reason to fear. Despite its different political philosophy, and our difficulties in the past, Guyana looks to us for understanding and cooperation."[12]

U.S. understanding and cooperation manifested itself in the largest U.S. aid package to Guyana, $24.8 million in 1978.[13] U.S. assistance to the Burnham government was again motivated by the desire to prevent more orthodox Marxist groups from seizing control of the government. The threat in the late 1970s came from Walter Rodney and the WPA. The WPA was calling for the removal of the PNC by any means necessary. Thousands of people were rallying in the parks and at street corners to hear Rodney and the other WPA leaders.[14] In this tense political atmosphere, the Carter administration chose to help Burnham rather than risk the possibility of a more radical socialist group acquiring control over the government. Nevertheless, U.S.-Guyana relations during the Carter presidency were never close.

The Reagan administration took a "cool but correct attitude" toward the Burnham regime. U.S. foreign aid was reduced to a trickle, and the Reagan administration did not extend the benefits of the Caribbean Basin Initiative to Guyana. U.S.-Guyana relations deteriorated rapidly in October 1983 over the issue of Grenada. The Burnham regime refused to participate in the invasion of Grenada and was especially opposed to U.S. participation in the operation.[15] Burnham may have also tipped off the ruling clique in Grenada about the imminent invasion. After the invasion, the Burnham government cosponsored, along with Nicaragua and Zimbabwe, a United Nations Security Council resolution condemning the invasion of Grenada by the United States and the seven Commonwealth Caribbean states. The resolution was blocked by the solitary vote of the United States, but a similar resolution in the General Assembly was approved by an overwhelming majority.[16] U S.-Guyana relations remained very strained up until Burnham's death in August 1985.

Shortly after Burnham's death, the new Guyanese president, Desmond Hoyte, initiated discussions with Washington in the hope of improving relations between the two countries.[17] The Hoyte regime was interested in receiving U.S. aid, particularly given the difficult economic conditions in Guyana. Progress in this direction depended on the willingness of the Hoyte regime to relinquish the "socialist revolution" at home. By 1987, the indications were clear that Hoyte was not as committed to socialist development as his predecessor. He avoids the socialist rhetoric and has opened up considerably to private enterprise. Relations between Guyana and the United States have improved. In fact, beginning in late 1986, the United States has been shipping wheat to Guyana under the PL 480 program.[18]

RELATIONS WITH VENEZUELA

Guyana's relations with Venezuela center on a dispute over territory. Venezuela is claiming three-fifths of the territory that now comprises Guyana. The current dispute between these two countries is a continuation of the Anglo-Venezuelan boundary dispute that had been settled by the Arbitration Tribunal in 1899. In 1962, the Venezuelan government expressed dissatisfaction with the 1899 arbitral award and based its dissatisfaction on historical documents which supposedly revealed the "inside story" behind the 1899 arbitral award by which the present boundary was laid.

The Anglo-Venezuelan boundary dispute, as it was then called, centered on 53,000 square miles of territory. Venezuela claimed that at independence, the territory ceded to her by Spain included the region in dispute. The British, on the other hand, claimed this territory as part of what was ceded to them by the Dutch. The British attempted to settle the issue in 1840 by a scientific survey of the boundary, but Venezuela rejected this result. On several occasions, Venezuela suggested that the matter should be settled by arbitration, but Britain would not accept arbitration. Venezuela tried to get the United States involved by charging that the Monroe Doctrine was being violated and, indeed, the United States took an active interest.[19] In 1897, the British and the Venezuelans eventually agreed to settle the matter by arbitration and both countries agreed to consider the award of the Tribunal of Arbitration as a "full, perfect and final settlement" of all questions referred to the arbitrators.[20]

The Arbitration Tribunal consisted of two British judges, two American judges, and a Russian jurist chosen by the other four as president of the Tribunal. The Venezuelan case was put forward by Benjamin Harrison, expresident of the United States. The Tribunal began its work on March 15, 1898, and the final award reached by unanimous decision was completed and signed on October 3, 1899. The prize of the award lay in the control of Point Barima, the strategic entrance of the Orinoco River. Venezuela obtained undisputed control of the Orinoco River Delta which included Point Barima. However, Great Britain received about 45,000 of the 53,000 square miles of disputed territory. Although the Venezuelans were disgruntled over the award, they participated in laying down the boundary according to the 1899 award. On January 10, 1905, representatives of Venezuela and Great Britain met in Georgetown, Guyana, and formally declared that the demarcation had been completed in accordance with the 1899 award.[21]

The Venezuelan declaration in 1962 that it would not abide by the 1899 arbitral award is based on a memorandum written by Severo Mallet-Prévost, a lawyer who had assisted Benjamin Harrison in the presentation of the Venezuelan case. The memorandum, published posthumously, alleged that the final judgment of the Arbitration Tribunal of 1899 was a diplomatic compromise, and that the compromise was reached after the president of the Arbitration Tribunal had threatened the American judges on the Tribunal that if they did not agree with the boundary line he proposed, he would side with the British judges. According to Mallet-Prévost, the American judges on the Tribunal were faced with a decision to lose everything and be content with filing a dissenting opinion or gain for Venezuela the portion of territory that commands over the mouth of the Orinoco River. With the concurrence of Benjamin Harrison, the American judges accepted the proposal of the president of the Tribunal. Mallet-Prévost claimed that he had been taken into confidence by the American judges on the Tribunal and had acted as a liaison between them and Benjamin Harrison. He concluded his memorandum with the opinion that Venezuela was dispossessed of territory to which Great Britain did not have any right whatsoever.[22]

The Mallet-Prévost memorandum was criticized long before it became the basis of the Venezuelan rejection of the 1899 arbitral award. One writer advanced a reasonable explanation of how the compromise was reached in 1899. In his desire to get unanimity, the president of the Tribunal probably pressured both the British and the American judges in the same way. The result was the compromise that he wanted and in which each party lost something.[23] Nevertheless, in 1962, the Venezuelan government chose to resuscitate its claim to Guyana's territory.

There are several plausible explanations of why Venezuela chose to resurrect its claim at this time. President Betancourt of Venezuela probably saw the border settlement as an issue assailing Venezuelan pride and honor and one that could beneficially serve to divert attention overseas while he proceeded with the task of establishing and consolidating representative government in Venezuela.[24] Further, by 1962, Guyana's independence from Britain was a foregone conclusion. The Betancourt government must have surmised that Great Britain would have invited international censure if she appeared to be abandoning this small country without first settling its boundary problem. Accordingly, the Venezuelan claim would be given the type of consideration it would not normally have received.[25] Finally, Venezuela shared a common goal with the United States in not wanting an independent socialist state on the continent of South America. Jagan was a close friend of Cuba's Fidel Castro and the Venezuelan military, which was fighting Castro-supported leftist insurgents internally, probably feared that an independent Guyana under Jagan might be used by Castro to ensure the victory of the insurgents. The border claim provided Venezuela with a mechanism for interfering in Guyana's affairs whenever it chose to do so.

Although Guyana was in a state of political turmoil when the Venezuelan claim was renewed in 1962, domestic political groups were unanimous in their rejection of the Venezuelan claim. However, since Guyana was still a colony, the formal response to Venezuela came from Britain. The British government rejected Venezuela's claim but indicated its preparedness to engage in a tripartite examination of all documents, British and Venezuelan, in order to dispel any doubts that the Venezuelan government might still have about the validity and propriety of the 1899 award.[26] For the first time, the Guyana government would be a party to the discussions concerning the disputed territory.

The documents on each side were examined between November 5, 1963, and December 12, 1963, and talks on the border question took place in London in December 1965, and in Geneva in February 1966. On February 17, 1966, Britain, Guyana, and Venezuela signed an agreement in Geneva, which provided for the establishment of a boundary commission, made up of two Guyanese and two Venezuelans, to seek a satisfactory solution of the controversy. If, after a period of four years, a full agreement had not been arrived at, the governments of Guyana and Venezuela agreed to choose one of the means of peaceful settlement provided in Article 33 of the United Nations Charter.[27]

Guyana became independent in May 1966, but the euphoria over independence was shattered in October by news that Venezuelan troops were shelling a Guyanese outpost across the border. Venezuelan troops then seized and occupied the eastern portion of the island of Ankoko on the Cuyuni River. This island had until then been under Guyanese control by virtue of the 1899 arbitral award. The Burnham government protested. The Venezuelan government insisted that the island was Venezuelan territory and kept it. What was especially shocking to the Guyana government was the fact that an international agreement was in force and that Venezuela chose to ignore that agreement and press its claims by force. The Guyana government feared that Venezuela would use its superior military force to incrementally occupy the disputed territory.

Relations between the two countries were very tense after the Ankoko affair. In January 1967, the Burnham government accused Venezuela of meddling in Guyana's internal affairs. The Burnham government claimed that the Second Secretary of the Venezuelan Embassy, Leopoldo Taylhardat, had been encouraging the Amerindians in Guyana, most of whom live in the disputed area, to revolt. The Burnham government expelled Taylhardat from Guyana.[28] The following month, Venezuela objected to Guyana becoming a signatory of the Treaty of Tlatelolco which banned nuclear weapons from South America. Later the same year, the Venezuelan government vetoed Guyana's attempt to become a member of the Organization of American States.[29]

The following year, the Venezuelan government began to apply new pressures against Guyana. The Burnham government's 1966–1972 development plan had placed a great amount of emphasis on attracting foreign investors into the country. To this end, the Burnham government was expending enormous sums on shaping and improving the national infrastructure. The Venezuelan government tried to sabotage Burnham's development program by discouraging foreign investors from entering the area. On June 15, 1968, the *Times* of London carried an advertisement by the Venezuelan government, which stated that Venezuela would not recognize any concessions granted by Guyana in the disputed area. On July 9, the Venezuelan president, Raúl Leoni, issued a decree by which he annexed to Venezuela the territorial waters lying along the coast of the disputed territory. The Venezuelan decree recognized Guyana's jurisdiction over all waters up to the three-mile limit off the coast, but pronounced Venezuelan jurisdiction over waters between the three-mile limit and the twelve-mile limit. Leoni indicated that the Venezuelan navy might be ordered to enforce this decree by patrolling these waters. The Guyana government protested fiercely. Although the waters were never patrolled by Venezuela, the decree had the effect of scaring off prospective investors who might have been interested in the mineral wealth of the region.[30]

In January 1969, the Venezuelan government encouraged an uprising in the Rupununi Savannas, in the southern part of Guyana. Two wealthy Guyanese ranchers, the Melvilles and the Harts, and some Amerindian followers attacked the town of Lethem on January 2 and killed several policemen. The rebellion was put down by the Guyana Defense Force and the rebels fled across the borders into Venezuela and Brazil. The Burnham government took the matter to the U.N. Security Council where it accused the Venezuelan government of engaging in subversive activities among Guyana's Amerindians. The Venezuelan government denied the allegation. However, on January 10, 1969, the Venezuelan minister of interior, Dr. Renaldo Leandro Mora, admitted that some Guyanese had received training in Venezuela, and that Venezuela would grant asylum to the rebels.[31]

After the Rupununi rebellion, Venezuelan pressures against Guyana lessened. This was largely the result of a successful diplomatic campaign conducted by Guyana's Foreign Affairs Ministry. Guyana's foreign minister, Sonny Ramphal, had been arguing in various international fora that most of the world's frontiers would be thrown into chaos if all that a party to a boundary settlement had to do was to claim that the settlement was not valid without being required to establish the truth of its claims. He cautioned that countries that have had frontier problems could not support Venezuela's claim without risking a reopening of their own boundary settlements.[32]

The persuasiveness of Ramphal's argument was demonstrated at the United Nations conference on the Law of Treaties during April and May of 1969. The Conference which reopened in Vienna on April 9 was intended to put finishing touches on a 75-article draft treaty designed to govern the international conduct of states. Article 42 of this treaty called for limitation on the right of each nation to invalidate or terminate treaties previously agreed to. The highlight of the April-May session was the Venezuelan effort to modify Article 42 and the Guyanese countereffort to prevent any such modification. Article 42 was eventually adopted without alteration. Venezuela discovered that several Latin American countries—Mexico, Argentina, Brazil, Peru and Panama—were not sympathetic to its arguments.[33]

After this diplomatic setback at Vienna, the Venezuelan government seemed willing to reach some sort of understanding with Guyana. With Trinidad's prime minister, Eric Williams, acting as an intermediary, Guyana and Venezuela began secret talks in Trinidad in February 1970. These talks were continued in Guyana and Venezuela. Eventually, on June 18, 1970, the foreign ministers of Venezuela and Guyana met in Port-of-Spain, Trinidad, and signed a new protocol to the Geneva Agreement. The Protocol of Port-of-Spain, as it is called, placed a moratorium on the dispute for a period of 12 years. The protocol was renewable automatically unless either party gave notice of its unwillingness to renew it.[34]

Relations between Guyana and Venezuela improved somewhat over the next few years. In March 1971, the Venezuelan minister of development visited Guyana and discussed trade possibilities between the two countries. The following month the Guyanese deputy prime minister reciprocated with a visit to Venezuela. In 1972, Venezuela participated in the Caribbean Festival of Arts hosted by Guyana. In 1974, the Guyanese foreign minister visited Venezuela and the following year, Guyana's prime minister made his first visit to Venezuela. As a result of these interactions, Venezuela began to import alumina from Guyana. In 1978, the Venezuelan government appeared willing to scale down its territorial claim to a quarter of the area originally claimed provided that Venezuela would get an outlet to the Atlantic Ocean.[35] The Burnham government was not very receptive to this idea.

With the moratorium on the dispute in effect, the Burnham government tried to populate the disputed area. It tried to encourage West Indians to settle there but this effort was unsuccessful. The government gave its approval to a settlement by the Rev. Jim Jones and the People's Temple. This ended in a well-publicized tragedy in November 1978. In 1980, the Burnham government was negotiating with the Christian Refugee Team International, a U.S.-based organization, on the possibility of establishing a settlement in the disputed area for Hmong refugees from Southeast Asia.[36] The plan came under attack from the domestic opposition party and also from Venezuela, and was cancelled.

In April 1981, President Burnham visited Venezuela at the urgent request of the Venezuelan president, Luis Herrera Campins. President Herrera notified Burnham that Venezuela would not extend the Protocol of Port-of-Spain when it expired in June 1982. Herrera also objected to the hydroelectric project that the Guyana government was constructing on the upper Mazaruni River in the disputed area. The Burnham government was alarmed by this objection since the hydroelectric project had been going on since 1972 and since the Burnham government had kept the Venezuelan government informed about the project. The Burnham government was worried that Venezuela might again be considering the use of force to dismember Guyana. In September 1981, the Burnham government complained to the U.N. General Assembly about Venezuela's efforts to subvert the economic development of the disputed area. The following year, Guyana complained to the Security Council about territorial violations by Venezuelan armed personnel.[37]

The Protocol of Port-of-Spain expired on June 18, 1982. Since no new agreements had been reached, and since the two countries could not agree on the means to resolve the dispute, they referred the matter to the secretary general of the United Nations, as required by the 1966 Geneva Agreement, for his recommendation of a means to resolve the dispute peacefully. In March 1983, the Burnham government accepted Venezuela's proposal that Secretary General Javier Pérez de Cuellar act as a mediator in the border dispute.[38]

In 1985, the *Catholic Standard* reported that the Guyana government was considering a proposal from Venezuela according to which Venezuela would drop its original claim if it could have a port on the Atlantic and a strip of coastal territory to link the port to Venezuela.[39] This raised hopes in Guyana that a final settlement to the border dispute was imminent. However, as this book goes to press, the issue remains unresolved.

The PNC government has always been afraid that Venezuela would use its superior military to enforce its territorial claim against Guyana. This fear has been fed by past Venezuelan actions including the seizure of Ankoko in 1966, the Leoni threat to patrol the waters off the Guyana coast, the Venezuelan role in the 1969 Rupununi uprising, and various border incidents. However, in 1982 when Argentina resorted to military means to settle its territorial dispute with Britain over the Falklands, the Guyana government felt that Venezuela had finally been provided the precedent it needed to invade.

When Argentina invaded the Falklands in 1982, Guyana and Venezuela found themselves on opposite sides of the issue. Guyana supported Britain in the crisis, while Venezuela strongly supported Argentina and, in fact, presented the Argentine case before the EEC countries. The Guyana government became afraid that Venezuela might adopt the Argentine solution to their border dispute. In fact, the use of force was proposed by several prominent Venezuelans including Miguel Angel Capríles, publisher of *El Mundo*.[40]

In April 1982, a report originating from Brazil indicated a buildup of Venezuelan troops on the border with Guyana and suggested an impending invasion. The Venezuelan ambassador to Guyana claimed that the troops were engaged in routine military exercises.[41] No invasion took place.

The Guyana government became even more fearful of a Venezuelan invasion after the U.S. invasion of Grenada. This was largely why Guyana felt such a strong need to protest the action in the United Nations. It was important to Guyana to bring international condemnation on the transgressors in order to despoil what might otherwise have appeared to the Venezuelan government as a propitious climate to advance its claims against Guyana by force of arms. Indeed, because of its socialist ideology, the Burnham government felt doubly threatened by the invasion. The invasion of Grenada revived memories of past U.S. actions against Guyana. Also, since socialist Guyana, like Grenada, had been excluded from receiving any of the benefits of the Caribbean Basin Initiative, the Burnham government feared that the U.S. action against Grenada presaged possible destabilization actions against it by either the United States, or by any of Guyana's neighbors not comfortable with the socialist path Guyana was taking. Venezuela seemed well qualified to be a proxy for the United States. Guyana was not invaded, but the fear lingers.

RELATIONS WITH BRAZIL

Although Guyana shares a 720-mile frontier with Brazil, there exists no border problem between these two countries. In fact, Brazil has been sympathetic to Guyana in its border dispute with Venezuela. Brazil is not happy about the prospect of Venezuela expanding by gobbling up over one-half of Guyana. However, Brazil's support to Guyana is based on the condition that Guyana does not accept military help from Cuba.

Brazil established an embassy in Guyana in 1968. It has provided both military and economic assistance to Guyana. Military assistance has included training in jungle warfare, parachuting, and military engineering. Brazil has agreed to sell military equipment to Guyana including troop carriers and reconnaissance aircraft. In 1971, Brazil offered to provide technical assistance to the Guyana government to construct a highway from Georgetown to Lethem, a town close to the Brazilian border. The Brazilian government plans to construct a road linking Lethem to the Brazilian town of Manaus. When the road is completed, Brazil hopes to have access to the Atlantic through the port at Georgetown. The Guyana government hopes to benefit from Brazil's use of the port at Georgetown. Nevertheless, the Guyana government declined Brazilian technical assistance and went about the 120-mile project by itself, though it has accepted lines of credit from Brazil for the purpose of road construction.[42]

The only tense period in Guyana-Brazilian relations was in 1976 when the Brazilian government believed that Guyana was hosting Cuban and Chinese troops. Brazil conducted military maneuvers, involving over two divisions, near its border with Guyana.[43] Since that time, however, relations between the two countries have been cordial, though Brazil continues to closely monitor Guyana-Cuban relations.

RELATIONS WITH SURINAM

Guyana also has a boundary dispute with Surinam, its eastern neighbor. The territory in question is located in the southeast corner of Guyana, between the Corentyne River and the New River. The New River Triangle, as it is called, is about 7,000 square miles and is believed to be rich in minerals.

The boundary dispute is almost as old as the one with Venezuela. The accepted boundary between Guyana and Surinam is the Corentyne River. However, in its upper course, the Corentyne River is fed by two branches. The British position had been that the easterly branch was the true Corentyne River and that everything to the west was British territory. The Dutch, on the other hand, insisted that the westerly branch was the true Corentyne River and that lands to the east of this branch were Dutch territory. The British and the Dutch had not resolved the issue by the time Guyana acquired its independence from Great Britain. In 1962, when the Venezuelan government resuscitated its claim, the Dutch government on behalf of its colony Surinam reopened the boundary question with Britain and Guyana.[44]

In August 1969, Surinam inserted a military unit into the New River Triangle, which was pushed out by the Guyana Defense Force. There was an exchange of gunfire, but there were no casualties.[45] The governments of Guyana and Surinam subsequently agreed to resume negotiations with a view to peacefully resolving the issue. Cordial relations prevailed between the two countries until the 1980s.

Strains in Guyana-Surinamese relations center on the issue of Guyanese immigration to Surinam. As political and economic conditions worsened in Guyana, thousands of Guyanese migrated to Surinam. Most of the migrants became involved in the rice industry in Surinam. In 1982, it was estimated that Guyanese immigrants accounted for approximately one-tenth of the population of Surinam. After the military takeover in Surinam in 1980, economic conditions began to deteriorate. The government of Colonel Desi Bouterse has turned its attention to the Guyanese immigrants. Relations between the two countries have been soured by stories of forcible repatriation of some of these immigrants.[46]

THE COMMONWEALTH CARIBBEAN

Soon after Burnham got into power, he began to push for integration with the other British Caribbean territories. Guyana had not been a member of the ill-fated West Indian Federation that lasted from 1958 to 1962. Burnham had been a strong advocate of membership for Guyana, but the Jagan government had resisted. On December 15, 1965, Guyana signed an agreement with Antigua and Barbados establishing the Caribbean Free Trade Association (CARIFTA). Since all of these entities were still colonies, the agreement remained unimplemented. The CARIFTA agreement underwent revision as additional territories decided to join and finally came into effect on May 1, 1968. Its membership included Guyana, Barbados, Antigua, and Trinidad-and-Tobago, all of which were independent by this time. By 1971, Dominica, Grenada, St. Kitts-Nevis, St. Lucia, St. Vincent, Jamaica, Monserrat, and Belize were members of CARIFTA. The administration of CARIFTA was to be handled by the Commonwealth Caribbean Regional Secretariat located in Georgetown, Guyana. CARIFTA members pledged to eliminate tariffs and quotas on each other's products. CARIFTA members were divided into two groups, the more developed and the less developed countries. The less developed countries were allowed to remove barriers to trade gradually.[47]

The founders of CARIFTA saw this as leading to Commonwealth Caribbean economic integration and eventually to political integration. In fact, in 1971 Guyana led an abortive attempt at political integration. On July 25, 1971, representatives of Guyana, Dominica, Grenada, St. Lucia, St. Kitts-Nevis, and St. Vincent met in Grenada and signed the Grenada Declaration, calling for the establishment of a new unified Caribbean state by 1973. However, Guyana was the only independent nation among the signatories. St. Lucia was reluctant to continue without Trinidad-and-Tobago and expressed concern about communist influence if Jagan's PPP returned to power in Guyana. Grenada also defected and the project was dropped.[48]

In October 1972, the CARIFTA heads of government met in Trinidad and agreed to establish a common market. In April 1973, at a follow-up conference in Georgetown, Guyana, the Georgetown Treaty formally established the Caribbean Common Market (CARICOM). The treaty was left open for signature until July 1, 1973, the hope being that most of the Commonwealth Caribbean countries could be induced to join. However, several of the CARIFTA members delayed joining CARICOM and on July 4, 1973, CARICOM was launched with only four members: Guyana, Jamaica, Trinidad, and Barbados. Most of the remaining CARIFTA members ratified the treaty by May 1, 1974.[49]

CARICOM is governed by the Conference of Heads of Government. The organization's objective is the economic integration of the member states. Tariffs among members were removed and a common external tariff was established. Through a Standing Committee of Ministers of Foreign Affairs, the member states hope to coordinate their foreign policies and to adopt common positions on major international issues.[50]

Guyana's entry into CARIFTA and CARICOM has been criticized by

Guyana's opposition leader Jagan who claims that the common market approach fits neatly into the "new strategy of U.S. imperialism." The elimination of tariff barriers in the region redounds to the benefit of U.S.-based multinational corporations with branch plants in countries such as Jamaica, Trinidad, and Barbados. Jagan also saw Guyana being relegated to the role of an agricultural producer while the rest of the West Indies became industrialized. What lent further ammunition to domestic critics of Guyana's involvement in CARICOM was the fact that in the first few years, Guyana's exports to its partners did not increase significantly, while Jamaica, Trinidad, and Barbados enjoyed significant export gains.[51]

CARICOM has been experiencing serious problems since 1973. The increases in oil prices caused grave economic problems for all of the member states, with the exception of oil-producing Trinidad. As a result, member states began reducing imports in an effort to redress serious balance of payments problems. CARICOM relations were also strained by the emergence of differing political ideologies. After 1970, the Guyana government described itself increasingly in socialist terms. Between 1972 and 1979, Jamaica was engaged in socialist experimentation. And in 1979, Maurice Bishop overthrew the Gairy government in Grenada and set up a socialist regime.

As a result of these developments, the annual meeting of the Caribbean heads of state did not take place between 1975 and 1982. In 1982, the Guyana government offered to host the heads of government meeting. Burnham had proposed to hold the meeting in the Essequibo region to which Venezuela has laid claim. Burnham had hoped that the meeting would demonstrate Caribbean support for Guyana in its dispute with Venezuela. Burnham was also interested in boosting his sagging prestige. Widely publicized reports of human rights violations, rigged elections, and possible complicity in the assassination of Guyanese historian Walter Rodney had damaged his reputation outside of the country. Largely because of this image, however, Caribbean heads of government were disinclined to meet in Guyana, and Guyana eventually withdrew the invitation.[52]

Relations between Guyana and the other Commonwealth Caribbean countries deteriorated rapidly after the U.S.-led invasion of Grenada in October 1983. The United States had been invited to participate in the invasion of Grenada by the Organization of Eastern Caribbean States, acting in consort with Jamaica and Barbados. All of these countries are members of CARICOM and, in fact, the decision to invade had been discussed at a CARICOM heads of state meeting two days before the invasion. At that meeting Forbes Burnham opposed the invasion proposal. After the invasion was launched, Burnham became openly critical of the CARICOM countries that joined with the United States in the invasion of Grenada. He referred to those governments as "lackeys" and "puppets."[53]

Several CARICOM heads of state, especially Tom Adams of Barbados, Edward Seaga of Jamaica, and Eugenia Charles of Dominica, were bitter about the Burnham stance on the Grenada invasion. Some of these heads of state even expressed the wish of forming a CARICOM 2 that would not include Guyana.[54] CARICOM has, nevertheless, weathered this crisis, and the death of Forbes Burnham might lead to a lessening of Guyana's isolation within the Commonwealth Caribbean.

AS A NONALIGNED STATE

In a March 1967 parliamentary debate on foreign policy, Burnham indicated that Guyana would link up with the nonaligned nations of the world. Concrete moves in this direction began in September 1969, when Guyana's foreign minister, S. S. Ramphal, was invited to participate in the meeting of foreign ministers of nonaligned nations at the United Nations headquarters. In September 1970, Guyana participated as a member at the summit conference of nonaligned nations in Lusaka, Zambia, and in August 1972, Guyana hosted the Conference of Foreign Ministers of Non-Aligned Countries.[55] Since that time, Guyana has played a very prominent role in the movement.

The PNC government chose membership in the Non-Aligned Movement to avoid entanglement in the East-West conflict. Foreign Minister Rashleigh Jackson described the Non-Aligned Movement as "a strategic alternative to a system premised on bloc politics."[56] Moreover, Guyana's world view has been shaped by a historical experience similar to that of most of the other members of the movement. Burnham alluded to this in his address to the 2nd biennial congress of the PNC in 1977 when he said:

As an ex-colony, raped and pauperised by imperialism, we are opposed to it in all its forms. We, therefore, support unequivocally the struggle of all peoples wherever they are, in Asia, Africa, or Latin America, to be free and independent. That is why even with our limited resources we have contributed sometimes until it hurts, to the freedom fighters in Southern Africa; that is why we are unapologetic in our opposition to the Pinochet regime in Chile and supported the Angolans in their war of liberation; that is why we help Zimbabwe and Namibia in tangible terms and give succour to displaced South African blacks. That explains, also, how the Vietnamese came to have our moral support.[57]

Apart from its strong support for liberation movements, the PNC government has taken other positions in international affairs that are in harmony with the general thrust of the Non-Aligned Movement. The

PNC government has supported the demand for a new international economic order. It has voted to regard Zionism as racism. It even broke diplomatic relations with Israel in 1974. It has opposed Israeli occupation of the Arab territories captured in the 1967 war and it supports the establishment of a homeland for the Palestinian people.[58]

The PNC government has worked tirelessly for international reaffirmation of the principle of nonintervention. Indeed, nonintervention has become a sacred principle of Guyanese international statecraft. This is because Guyana depends very much on the international community to restrain its predatory neighbor, Venezuela, from resorting to force. The Burnham government not only used the principle of nonintervention to condemn the U.S. invasion of Grenada, but also to support the Sandinistas in Nicaragua in their efforts "to defend and consolidate their revolution."[59] Guyana has found strong support within the Non-Aligned Movement for the principle of nonintervention.

Membership of the Non-Aligned Movement has conferred great benefits on the Guyana government. Most of the member states have socialist or left-leaning governments, and as the PNC embarked on a socialist path, it looked to member states for support. Burnham was greatly aware of the U.S. actions against his predecessor and he hoped to forestall any such action by whatever diplomatic support he could muster in the Non-Aligned Movement. The PNC government used the nonaligned conferences to complain about destabilization efforts against it. Because of Guyana's high visibility in the movement, the PNC was able to get the attention and support of member states. Burnham was acknowledging both the threat and the support when he said, "Even though we did not seek to export revolution, we were marked down for punitive action. As leading members of the Non-Aligned Movement, we received moral support from our colleagues."[60]

Perhaps the greatest benefit deriving from Guyana's membership in the Non-Aligned Movement relates to Guyana's border problem with Venezuela. The centrality of this issue to Guyana's international relations was underscored by Foreign Minister Rashleigh Jackson in an address to the U.N. General Assembly on October 5, 1983, when he said, "The struggle to preserve my country's territorial integrity never ceases to engage the energies and the attention of the Government and people of Guyana because of the untenable claim which Venezuela has been actively pursuing to over two-thirds of my country."[61] Guyana has used every international forum to present its case, but in the Non-Aligned Movement, Guyana has had tremendous success because the member states support Guyana against Venezuela, which is not a member of the movement. In early 1983, when Venezuela applied for membership in the Non-Aligned Movement, Guyana opposed the application on the ground that Venezuela would not renounce the use of force as required by the movement. The objection was based on Venezuela's dissenting vote on a 1981 declaration introduced by Guyana and adopted by the U.N. General Assembly that condemned intervention and interference in the internal affairs of states. Venezuela withdrew its application in February 1983. At the New Delhi summit meeting of the nonaligned states, Guyana received support for its position on the border issue with Venezuela.[62]

There is no question that Guyana's behavior within the United Nations and within the Non-Aligned Movement earned it a great amount of respect within the Third World. However, as human rights violations and other acts of repression became publicized, the international image of the Burnham government became somewhat tarnished. The assassination of the noted Third World historian, Walter Rodney, was particularly damaging and drew even more attention to Guyana's domestic politics. Burnham's death has provided his heirs with an opportunity to reclaim a more respectable standing within the Third World. Whether they avail themselves of this opportunity will depend in part on their willingness to disassociate themselves from the repression that became synonymous with the Burnham regime.

NOTES

1. Agency for International Development, *Volume II Latin America and Caribbean: Overseas Loans and Grants and Assistance from International Organizations: Obligations and Authorizations, 1946–1983* (Washington, D.C.: Agency for International Development, 1984).

2. Premdas, "Guyana: Socialist Reconstruction or Political Opportunism?" p. 136.

3. Agency for International Development, *Volume II Latin America and Caribbean*.

4. Premdas, "Guyana: Communal Conflict, Socialism and Political Reconciliation," p. 71.

5. Manley, *Guyana Emergent*, pp. 68–69.

6. *Ibid.*, p. 71. See also W. Raymond Duncan, "Caribbean Leftism," *Problems of Communism* (May-June, 1978), p. 43.

7. Manley, *Guyana Emergent*, pp. 68–69.

8. Premdas, "Guyana: Communal Conflict, Socialism and Political Reconciliation," p. 72.

9. "Guyana Mourns 11 Dead comrades," *Caribbean Contact* (November 1976), p. 24.

10. *Ibid.*

11. Anthony P. Maingot, "The Difficult Path to Socialism in the English-Speaking Caribbean," in Richard Fagen, ed. *The State in United States-Latin American Relations* (Stanford: Stanford University Press, 1979), pp. 297–298.

12. *Ibid.*, p. 274.

13. Agency for International Development, *Volume II Latin America and Caribbean*.

14. Joseph B. Treaster, "Guyana's President Facing Biggest Challenge in 15 Years," *New York Times*, October 13, 1979.

15. "Guyana's Strong Anti-Invasion Stand," *Caribbean Contact* (December 1983), p. 3; "Moscow Eyes Guyana," *Backgrounder* (Washington, D.C.: The Heritage Foundation, 1986), pp. 7–8.

16. "Grenada: More Light on it," *The Economist* (November 5, 1983), pp. 41–42.

17. "Guyana Politics: High hopes on U.S. help," *Latin American Weekly Report* (26 June 1986), p. 3.

18. "Wheat Coming, So Flour Goes," *Catholic Standard*, August 31, 1986, pp. 1, 4; *Address By His Excellency, Cde. H. D. Hoyte, S.C.*, p. 14.

19. Marcus Baker, "The Anglo-Venezuelan Boundary Dispute," *The National Geographic Magazine* 11 (April 1900), pp. 131–132.

20. Braveboy-Wagner, *The Venezuela-Guyana Border Dispute*, p. 106.

21. Baker, "The Anglo-Venezuelan Boundary Dispute," p. 141. See also Leslie B. Rout, *Which Way Out? An Analysis of the Venezuela/Guyana Border Dispute* (East Lansing, Michigan: Michigan State University, 1971), p. 19.

22. Otto Schoenrich, "The Venezuela-British Guiana Boundary Dispute," *American Journal of International Law* xxxxiii (July 1949), pp. 523–530.

23. William Cullen Dennis, "The Venezuela-British Guiana Boundary Arbitration of 1899," *American Journal of International Law* xxxxiv (October 1950), pp. 724–726.

24. For an examination of domestic political conditions in Venezuela during this period, see David E. Blank, *Politics in Venezuela* (Boston: Little, Brown and Company, 1973), pp. 109–117.

25. H. J. M. Hubbard, *The Venezuela Border Issue and the Occupation of Ankoko* (Georgetown: New Guyana Co. Ltd., 1967), p. 30.

26. *Ibid.*, pp. 11–17.

27. "Appendix C: The Geneva Agreement," in Braveboy-Wagner, *The Venezuela-Guyana Border Dispute*, pp. 324–326.

28. Hubert Williams, "9,000 Sq. Miles Of Land For Guyana's Amerindians," *Caribbean Contact* (April 1976), p. 17.

29. Rout, *Which Way Out?*, pp. 61–62.

30. *Ibid.*, p. 63. See also Forbes Burnham, "Statement in National Assembly on Guyana/Venezuela Relations, 12 July 1968," in Nascimento and Burrowes, eds., *A Destiny to Mould*, pp. 167–70.

31. Rout, *Which Way Out?*, pp. 65–66. See also Forbes Burnham, "Radio Broadcast to the nation on disturbances in the Rupununi Savannahs, 4 January 1969," in Nascimento and Burrowes, ed., *Destiny to Mould*, pp. 171–176.

32. Rout, *Which Way Out?*, p. 36.

33. *Ibid.*, p. 67.

34. "Appendix D: The Protocol of Port-of-Spain," Braveboy-Wagner, *The Venezuela-Guyana Border Dispute*, pp. 327–329.

35. *Ibid.*, pp. 184–185.

36. "Refugees Plan Now Cancelled," *Caribbean Contact* (June 1980), p. 9.

37. Braveboy-Wagner, *The Venezuela-Guyana Border Dispute*, pp. 235–237. See

also "Venezuelan Aggression: President Burnham's Stand," *Caribbean Contact* (May 1981), pp. 5, 19.

38. "Guyana/USA," *Latin American Weekly Report* (March 31, 1983), p. 12.

39. "Burnham On The Border," *Catholic Standard*, April 21, 1985, pp. 1, 3.

40. Braveboy-Wagner, *The Venezuela-Guyana Border Dispute*, p. 232–233.

41. *Ibid.*

42. Braveboy-Wagner, *The Venezuela-Guyana Border Dispute*, p. 208.

43. "Burnham's Borders 'headaches': Undermining Socialism?" *Caribbean Contact* (July 1976), pp. 12–13.

44. Manley, *Guyana Emergent*, pp. 42–44.

45. Nascimento and Burrowes, eds., *A Destiny to Mould*, pp. 177–179.

46. Clive Thomas, "Collapse of Guyana's Economy," p. 5. See also Guyana Human Rights Association, *Guyana Human Rights Report 1985*, p. 39.

47. Manley, *Guyana Emergent*, pp. 28–29. See also G. Pope Atkins, *Latin America in the International Political System* (New York: The Free Press, 1976), pp. 299–300.

48. Atkins, *Latin America*, p. 300; Braveboy-Wagner, *The Venezuela-Guyana Border Dispute*, pp. 213–214.

49. Atkins, *Latin America*, p. 301.

50. *Ibid.*

51. Manley, *Guyana Emergent*, p. 32.

52. Braveboy-Wagner, *The Venezuela-Guyana Border Dispute*, p. 215.

53. "U S. Forces Sweep Grenada," *Caribbean Contact* (November 1983), p. 2.

54. "Hope For Poor From Nassau Summit?" *Caribbean Contact* (August 1984), p. 3.

55. Manley, *Guyana Emergent*, pp. 65–66.

56. Rashleigh E. Jackson, *Prospects For International Cooperation* (Georgetown: Guyana National Printers Ltd., 1983), p. 20.

57. Burnham, *Economic Liberation Through Socialism*, p. 29.

58. Rashleigh E. Jackson, *Multilateralism: A Prerequisite For An Ordered International System* (Georgetown: Design & Graphics Limited, 1984), p. 35; Jagan, "Report of the Central Committee . . . ," p. 29.

59. Jackson, *Prospects For International Co-operation*, p. 7.

60. Burnham, *Economic Liberation Through Socialism*, p. 29.

61. Jackson, *Prospects For International Co-operation*, p. 30.

62. Braveboy-Wagner, *The Venezuela-Guyana Border Dispute*, pp. 223, 239–240.

7

CONCLUSION

Guyana is the only country within the Commonwealth Caribbean that has abandoned the Westminster system of government. With Grenada back on the road to constitutional democracy, Guyana remains the only authoritarian state in CARICOM. The ruling party insists on its paramountcy over all other national institutions. It even requires the security forces to take a pledge of loyalty to the party. And it justifies its uninterrupted stay in office on the basis of victories in elections that are dishonest.

Guyana resembles its Latin neighbors in at least one respect, in the existence of a personalistic leadership tradition. Guyanese politics have been dominated by two men, Forbes Burnham and Cheddi Jagan, each of whom commanded the allegiance of one of Guyana's two major ethnic groups. The more dominating personality by far was Forbes Burnham. Until his death, all of the strands of state power converged on his person. The new constitution promulgated in 1980 merely rationalized this concentration of state power. Based on the criterion of political longevity, Burnham will be remembered as one of the Third World's ablest politicians. His political longevity rested on his success in neutralizing the numerical advantage that his arch-rival Jagan derived from Indian support. In addition, Burnham's public embrace of socialism placed him in a position to outflank Jagan. He proceeded to implement policies that Jagan had long advocated. Burnham's ideological stance led to fraternal links with foreign socialist leaders and an enlarged reputation within the socialist world. Eventually, Jagan had little choice but to support Burnham with hope of pushing the latter even further to the left.

However, the supporting argument for cooperative socialism lacked internal consistency and ultimately relied on coercion. At the economic level, the emphasis on cooperatives was touted not only as the best way to set Guyana on a noncapitalist development path but also as a way of maximizing the participation of the masses. At the political level, the PNC's advocacy of the principle of party paramountcy negated mass political participation. In its enforcement of this principle, the party infringed on the civil rights of Guyanese and caused some segments of the Christian Church to align themselves with the traditional opposition.

The PNC's longevity in office did not advance the country along the path of economic development or national reconciliation. The economic results of the policies followed under cooperative socialism were disastrous for the country. For about a decade the economy experienced negative growth rates. Food shortages have been widespread and health care has plummeted. Emigration from Guyana has become a mentality. Both blacks and Indians leave Guyana out of frustration with the privations that attend day-to-day living, though many Indians also feel that they have been relegated to the status of second-class citizens. The result is that Guyana has been suffering a hemorrhage of skilled personnel. Considering the declining domestic standards in education, it appears as though the damage caused by this exodus will not be remedied in the short term.

Any analysis of Guyanese politics must recognize the ethnic bifurcation of the society. Ethnic relations between the Indians and the blacks degenerated into open confrontation in the early 1960s. While no similar confrontations have recurred, ethnic suspicions and ethnic tensions persist because of the nature of party politics wherein the PPP and the PNC are perceived to represent the Indians and the blacks respectively and also because of the division of labor that has emerged in Guyanese society in which Indians predominate in agriculture and the private sector while blacks control most of the positions of public authority in the country.

Publicly, both the PPP and the PNC have emphasized class cleavages while accusing each other of exploiting racial divisions. Privately, however, both of these parties have expended considerable effort to cultivate and consolidate their respective ethnic followings. The PPP has successfully warded off challenges to its hold over the Indians by warning Indians that newer parties would "split the vote," meaning the Indian vote, even though at the national level, the party argues that voting in Guyana is meaningless because the elections are rigged. Nevertheless, the WPA and even some of the newer parties have been attracting Indians into their fold. The PNC, on the other hand, has always assumed the support of Afro-Guyanese and has used the patronage potential of the state to maintain this support. However, deteriorating economic conditions in the late 1970s and the emergence of the WPA as a contender for the black vote seriously threatened the PNC's continuation in office. As its African support base thinned, the PNC resorted to carefully staged attacks on Indians in order to repolarize the situation in Guyana and to quietly remind blacks that it was the best guarantor of their protection. Since PNC rule has ultimately depended on the support of the predominantly black military, the party strategy seemed to be one of convincing the army leadership in particular that the party best represented black interests.

Ironically, the greatest threat to the continuation of PNC rule may not be the PPP or the WPA but the army. Under Forbes Burnham, the Guyana Defense Force became an adjunct of the PNC. Burnham insisted that the GDF pledge its allegiance to the PNC. Burnham also used the GDF to aid the party in securing electoral victories. However, loyalty to the PNC was tacitly understood by the military to mean loyalty to Forbes Burnham. Burnham was charismatic and his reputation as a scholar and orator overawed the officer corps of the GDF. As long as Burnham controlled the PNC, the GDF made no attempt to challenge the party. The 1985 election has shown that the PNC continues to rely on the GDF to maintain it in power. The officers in control of the GDF are young and ambitious. The question that the new party leader, Desmond Hoyte, must be pondering is how long he can rely on army support. Hoyte does not have the charisma for which Burnham was famous, and Hoyte inherited a host of economic and social problems for which there are no quick solutions. Yet Burnham's death provided Hoyte with the opportunity to break with some of the old PNC practices, both ideological and coalitional, and in the latter regard to try to establish a bridge to the Indians in Guyana. As this book goes to press, there are signs that Hoyte is moving on these fronts. Naturally, the military will continue to play a prominent role in Guyanese politics. However, the temptation for it to seize power in Guyana will be inversely proportional to Hoyte's success in broadening his support base within the Guyanese population, assuming that he is simultaneously able to ward off internal challenges to his leadership of the party.

BIBLIOGRAPHY

Adamson, Alan H. *Sugar With Slaves: The Political Economy of British Guiana, 1838–1904*. New Haven: Yale University Press, 1972.

Agee, Philip. *Inside the Company: CIA Diary*. London: Penguin Books, 1975.

Agency for International Development, *Volume II Latin America and Caribbean: Overseas Loans and Grants and Assistance from International Organizations: Obligations and Authorizations, 1946–1983*. Washington, D.C.: Agency for International Development, 1984.

Anglin, Douglas G. "The Political Development of the West Indies," in David Lowenthal, ed., *The West Indies Federation*. New York: Columbia University Press, 1961.

Atkins, G. Pope. *Latin America in the International Political System*. New York: The Free Press, 1976.

Avebury, Lord, and the British Parliamentary Human Rights Group, "Guyana's 1980 Elections: The Politics of Fraud," *Caribbean Review* 10 (Spring 1981): 8–11, 44.

Baber, Colin, and Henry B. Jeffrey. *Guyana: Politics, Economics and Society*. Boulder: Lynne Rienner Publishers, Inc., 1986.

Baker, Marcus. "The Anglo-Venezuelan Boundary Dispute," *The National Geographic Magazine* 11 (April 1900): 128–144.

Barnet, Richard J. *Intervention and Revolution*. New York: New American Library, 1972.

Beachey, R. W. *The British West Indies Sugar Industry in the Late 19th Century*. Oxford: Basil Blackwell, 1957.

Braveboy-Wagner, Jacqueline. *The Venezuela-Guyana Border Dispute*. Boulder: Westview Press, 1984.

British Guiana Suspension of Constitution, United Kingdom Government White Paper. British Guiana: Bureau of Public Information, 1953.

Burnham, L. F. S. *Declaration of Sophia*. Georgetown: Guyana Printers Ltd., 1974.

Burnham, L. F. S. *Towards the Socialist Revolution*. Georgetown: Guyana Printers Ltd., 1975.

Burnham, L. F. S. *Economic Liberation Through Socialism*. Georgetown: Guyana Printers Ltd., 1977.

Burnham, L. F. S. *Towards The People's Victory*. Ruimveldt: Guyana Printers Ltd., 1979.

Chandisingh, Ranji. *Education in the Revolution for Socialist Transformation and Development*. Ruimveldt: Guyana Printers Ltd., 1979.

Chase, Ashton. *A History of Trade Unionism in Guyana 1900 to 1961*. Ruimveldt: New Guyana Company Ltd., 1964.

Clementi, Sir Cecil. *A Constitutional History of British Guiana*. London: Macmillan and Co. Ltd., 1937.

Constitution of the Co-operative Republic of Guyana. Ruimveldt: Guyana National Lithographic Co. Ltd., 1980.

Cummings, Leslie P. *Geography of Guyana*. London: Collins, 1976.

Danns, George K. "The Role of the Military in the National Security of Guyana," in Alma H. Young and Dion E. Phillips, eds., *Militarization in the Non-Hispanic Caribbean*. Boulder: Lynne Rienner Publishers, Inc., 1986.

Dennis, William Cullen. "The Venezuela-British Guiana Boundary Arbitration of 1899," *American Journal of International Law* XXXXIV (October 1950): 720–727.

Despres, Leo A. *Cultural Pluralism and Nationalist Politics in British Guiana*. Chicago: Rand McNally and Company, 1967.

Greene, J. E. *Race vs. Politics in Guyana*. Kingston: Institute of Social and Economic Research, University of the West Indies, 1974.

Guyana Human Rights Association. *Human Rights Report, Jan. 1980-June 1981*. Georgetown: Guyana Human Rights Association, 1981.

Guyana Human Rights Association. *Guyana Human Rights Report 1985*. Georgetown: Guyana Human Rights Association, 1985.

Halperin, Ernst. "Racism and Communism in British Guiana," *Journal of Interamerican Studies* 7 (January 1965), 95–134.

Hope, Kempe R. *The Post-War Planning Experience in Guyana*. Tempe: Center for Latin American Studies, Arizona State University, 1978.

Hope, Kempe R. *Guyana: Politics and Development in an Emergent Socialist State*. Cincinnati: Mosaic Press, 1986.

Hubbard, H. J. M. *Race and Guyana*. Georgetown: The Daily Chronicle, 1969.

Hubbard, H. J. M. *Venezuela Border Issue and Occupation of Ankoko*. Georgetown: New Guiana Co. Ltd., 1967.

Irving, Brian., ed. *Guyana*. Hato Rey: Inter-American University Press, 1972.

Jackson, Rashleigh E. *Prospects for International Co-operation*. Georgetown: Guyana National Printers Ltd., 1983.

Jackson, Rashleigh E. *Multilateralism: A Prerequisite for an Ordered International System*. Georgetown: Design & Graphics Ltd., 1984.

Jagan, Cheddi. *Forbidden Freedom*. New York: International Publishers Co. Inc., 1954.

Jagan, Cheddi. *The Anatomy of Poverty in Guyana*. Georgetown: New Guyana Company Ltd., 1964.

Jagan, Cheddi. *The West on Trial*. Berlin: Seven Seas Publishers, 1975.

Jagan, Cheddi. "Report of the Central Committee to the 19th Congress of the PPP," in *Documents of the 19th Congress, People's Progressive Party*. Georgetown: The New Guyana Company Ltd., 1976.

Jagan, Janet. *An Examination of National Service*. Georgetown: New Guyana Company Ltd., 1977.

Jayawardena, Chandra. *Conflict and Solidarity in a Guianese Plantation*. London: The Athlone Press, 1963.

Klineman, George, Sherman Butler, and David Conn. *The Cult That Died*. New York: G. P. Putnam's Sons, 1980.

Knowles, William H. *Trade Union Development and Industrial Relations in the British West Indies*. Berkeley: University of California Press, 1959.

Kwayana, Eusi. *Walter Rodney*. Georgetown: Working People's Alliance, 1986.

The Laws of Guyana: The Constitution. Georgetown: Guyana Lithographic Co. Ltd., 1973.

Lewis, Gordon K. *The Growth of the Modern West Indies*. New York: Monthly Review Press, 1968.

Mahant, E. E. "The Strange Fate of a Liberal Democracy," *The Round Table* 265 (January 1977): 77–89.

Maingot, Anthony P. "The Difficult Path to Socialism in the English-Speaking Caribbean," in Richard R. Fagen, ed., *The State in United States—Latin American Relations*. Stanford: Stanford University Press, 1979.

Manley, Robert H. *Guyana Emergent: The Post-Independence Struggle for Nondependent Development*. Cambridge, Mass.: Shenkman Publishing Company, Inc., 1982.

Marchetti, V., and J. D. Marks. *The CIA and The Cult of Intelligence*. New York: Dell Publishing Co., 1975.

Mazrui, Ali A., and Michael Tidy. *Nationalism and New States in Africa*. Portsmouth: Heinemann Educational Books, Inc., 1985.

Milne, R. S. "Guyana's Cooperative Republic," *Parliamentary Affairs* 28 (Autumn 1975): 347–367.

Naipaul, Shiva. *Journey To Nowhere: A New World Tragedy*. New York: Simon and Schuster, 1981.

Nath, Dwarka. *A History of Indians in Guyana*. London: Butler & Tanner Ltd., 1970.

National Unity for Democracy, Peace and Social Progress: Report of the Central Committee to the 22nd Congress of the People's Progressive Party. Annandale: People's Progressive Party, 1985.

Premdas, Ralph R. "Guyana: Communal Conflict, Socialism and Political Reconciliation," *Inter-American Economic Affairs* 30 (Spring 1977): 63–83.

Premdas, Ralph R. "Guyana: Socialist Reconstruction or Political Opportunism?" *Journal of Interamerican Studies and World Affairs* 20 (May 1978): 133–164.

Radosh, Ronald. *American Labor and United States Foreign Policy*. New York: Random House, 1969.

Reno, Phillip. *The Ordeal of British Guiana*. New York: Monthly Review Press, 1964.

Reston, James, Jr. *Our Father Who Art In Hell*. New York: Times Books, 1981.

Robertson, Sir James. *Report of the British Guiana Constitutional Commission*. London: His Majesty's Stationery Office, 1954.

Rodney, Walter. *The Struggle Goes On!* Georgetown: Working People's Alliance, 1979.

Rodney, Walter. *In Defence of Arnold Rampersand*. Georgetown: Working People's Alliance, 1982.

Rodway, James. *Guiana: British, Dutch and French*. London: T. Fisher Urwin, 1912.

Rout, Leslie B., Jr. *Which Way Out?* East Lansing: Michigan State University, 1971.

Ruhoman, Peter. *Centenary History of the East Indians in British Guiana, 1838–1938*. Georgetown: The Daily Chronicle Ltd., 1946.

Sackey, James A. "Dependence, Underdevelopment and Socialist-Oriented Transformation in Guyana," *Inter-American Economic Affairs* 33 (Summer 1969): 29–50.

Schlesinger, Arthur Jr. *A Thousand Days*. New York: Houghton Mifflin Co., 1965.

Schoenrich, Otto. "The Venezuela-British Guiana Boundary Dispute," *American Journal of International Law* XXXXIII (July 1949): 523–530.

Searwar, L., ed. *Cooperative Republic Guyana 1970*. Georgetown: Guyana Lithographic Co. Ltd., 1970.

Simms, Peter. *Trouble in Guyana*. London: George Allen and Urwin Ltd., 1966.

Sires, Ronald. "British Guiana: The Suspension of the Constitution," *Western Political Quarterly* 7 (December 1954): 554–569.

Smith, Raymond T. *British Guiana*. London: Oxford University Press, 1962.

Spinner, Thomas J., Jr. *A Political and Social History of Guyana, 1945–1983*. Boulder: Westview Press, 1984.

Springer, Hugh. "Federation in the Caribbean: An Attempt that Failed," in David Lowenthal and Lambros Comitas, eds., *The Aftermath of Sovereignty*. New York: Anchor Press, 1973.

Swan, Michael. *British Guiana*. London: Her Majesty's Stationery Office, 1957.

Thomas, Clive. *Hoyte's Economic Dynamism: Can It Work?* Georgetown: Working People's Alliance, 1986.

Thompson, Edgar T. "The Plantation Cycle and Problems of Typology," in Vera Rubin, ed., *Caribbean Studies: A Symposium*. Mona, Jamaica: Institute of Social and Economic Research, University of the West Indies, 1957.

United Nations. *1985 International Trade Statistics Yearbook. Volume I*. New York: United Nations, 1987.

Venn, J. A. *Report of a Commission of Inquiry Into the Sugar Industry of British Guiana*. London: His Majesty's Stationery Office, 1949.

Wagley, Charles. "Plantation America: A Culture Sphere," in Vera Rubin, ed., *Caribbean Studies: A Symposium*. Mona, Jamaica: Institute of Social and Economic Research, University of the West Indies, 1957.

Working People's Alliance. *Arguments For Unity Against The Dictatorship in Guyana*. Georgetown: Working People's Alliance, 1983.

The World Bank. *Guyana: A Framework for Economic Recovery*. Washington, D.C.: The World Bank, 1985.

INDEX

Accabre College, 50
Adams, Paula, 84
American Institute for Free Labor Development (AIFLD), 32
Amos, Linda, 83, 84
Anglo-Venezuelan boundary dispute, 123–25
Association for Social and Cultural Relations with Africa (ASCRIA), 46, 54, 55
Ato, Bilal, 85–86

bauxite exports: barter agreements involving, 107; decline in, 105, 108; declining quality of, 110; supply problems, 108, 110
bauxite industry, 108–11; control of, before nationalization, 110; declining production, 105, 107, 110; nationalization of, 110
bauxite miners: alienated from PNC, 56; hostile to PNC government, 92; supporting WPA, 55–56
Benn, Brindley, 25–26, 34–35, 50, 55
Berbice Mining Enterprise (BERMINE), 110
Best, Oswald, 96
Bhagwan, Moses, 50, 54
Bishop, Maurice, 133
blacks: activities dominated by, 8; appealed to by Burnham, 27; dominating GDF, GNS and Guyana Police Force, 77, 79; fearing Indian domination, 28; gang violence against Indians, 86–88; in House of

Israel, 85; joining PNC, 27; receiving best training in People's Militia, 81; represented by LCP, 13–14; resigning from PPP, 26–27; supporting WPA, 495
Bollers, Howard, 84
Booker Brothers McConnell & Co. Ltd., 6–7, 111; nationalization of, 27, 52
Bowman, Fred, 25
Brazil: relations with Guyana, 130
British Guiana East Indian Association (BGEIA), 14
British Guiana Labor Union (BGLU), 14–15, 23
budget deficits, 108
budget of 1962: opposition to, 30
budget of 1987, 116
Burnham, Linden Forbes Sampson, 22; appointing GDF officers, 77, 79; against Grenada Invasion, 133; assuming title of president, 75–76; attempting control of PPP, 25–26; attracting Portuguese to PNC, 27–28; as BGLU president, 23; committed to independence, 28; death of, 48; early career, 19; and formation of PPP, 19–20; Guyanese politics dominated by, 139; heckled by strikers, 92; helped by CIA, 45; insisting on elections before independence, 30, 31; insisting on ombudsman, 71; leadership struggles following death, 48–49; making himself commander-in-chief,

ABOUT THE AUTHOR

CHAITRAM SINGH is an assistant professor of political science at Berry College, Mt. Berry, GA. Born in Guyana, he holds a B.S. from the United States Military Academy, West Point, and an M.A. and a Ph.D. from the University of Florida. He served as an officer of the Guyana Defense Force and was an assistant professor in the Department of Government and International Studies at the University of South Carolina.

POLITICS IN LATIN AMERICA
A HOOVER INSTITUTION
SERIES
Robert Wesson, Series Editor

POLITICS IN CENTRAL AMERICA: Guatemala, El Salvador, Honduras, Costa Rica
Thomas P. Anderson

SOCIALISM, LIBERALISM, AND DICTATORSHIP IN PARAGUAY
Paul H. Lewis

PANAMANIAN POLITICS: From Guarded Nation to National Guard
Steve C. Ropp

BOLIVIA: Past, Present, and Future of its Politics
Robert J. Alexander

U.S. INFLUENCE IN LATIN AMERICA IN THE 1980s
Robert Wesson

DEMOCRACY IN LATIN AMERICA: Promise and Problems
Robert Wesson

MEXICAN POLITICS: The Containment of Conflict
Martin C. Needler

DEMOCRACY IN COSTA RICA
Charles D. Ameringer

NEW MILITARY POLITICS IN LATIN AMERICA
Robert Wesson

BRAZIL IN TRANSITION
Robert Wesson and David V. Fleischer

VENEZUELA: Politics in a Petroleum Republic
David E. Blank

HAITI: Political Failures, Cultural Successes
Brian Weinstein and Aaron Segal

GEOPOLITICS OF THE CARIBBEAN: Ministates in a Wider
World
Thomas D. Anderson

PUERTO RICO: Equality and Freedom at Issue
Juan M. Garcia-Passalacqua

LATIN AMERICA AND WESTERN EUROPE: Reevaluating
the Atlantic Triangle
Wolf Grabendorff and Riordan Roett

GEOPOLITICS AND CONFLICT IN SOUTH
AMERICA: Quarrels
Among Neighbors
Jack Child

LATIN AMERICAN VIEWS OF U.S. POLICY
Robert Wesson

CLASS, STATE, AND DEMOCRACY IN JAMAICA
Carl Stone

THE MEXICAN RULING PARTY: Stability and Authority
Dale Story

THE POLITICS OF COLOMBIA
Robert H. Dix

THE POLITICS OF EXTERNAL INFLUENCE IN THE DOMINICAN REPUBLIC
Michael J. Kryzanek and Howard J. Wiarda